# DEVELOPING YOUR SMALL CHURCH'S POTENTIAL

CARL S. DUDLEY
DOUGLAS ALAN WALRATH

DOUGLAS ALAN WALRATH
GENERAL EDITOR

Judson Press ® Valley Forge

Developing Your Small Church's Potential
Copyright © 1988
Judson Press, Valley Forge, PA 19482-0851

**Library of Congress**
Library of Congress Cataloging-in-Publication Data

Dudley, Carl S., 1932–
    Developing your small church's potential / Carl S. Dudley, Douglas Alan Walrath.
        p. cm.—(Small church in action)
    Includes bibliographical references.
    ISBN 0-8170-1120-X
    1. Small churches. I. Walrath, Douglas Alan, 1933– .
    II. Title. III. Series.
    BV637.8.D82 1988                                    88-12927
    254—dc19                                            CIP

10 09 08 07 06 05 04 03 02 01 00 99 98

6 5 4 3

Printed in the U.S.A.

# Foreword

S mall churches are in a class by themselves. To overlook that uniqueness is to misunderstand them.

Unfortunately, small churches are commonly misunderstood. For example, they have long been viewed as proving grounds for new pastors. According to that assumption, beginning pastors should make their mistakes in small churches; fewer people are involved and, therefore, the mistakes will be less costly. Also, those who demonstrate their ability in ministry with small churches will likely be effective pastors of larger churches.

Such viewpoints are hardly warranted. Only the most crass perspective could hold that those who are members of small churches deserve consistently lower quality, less experienced pastoral care than those who are members of large churches. Small churches are not smaller versions of large churches. They are qualitatively, as well as quantitatively, different. Nor do the insights that pastors gain in ministry with small congregations transfer directly to larger congregations. In my own experience those who minister well and are happy in small churches rarely are as happy or effective when they move to large churches. Church members who are nurtured and who are effective lay leaders in small churches rarely find similar nurture or are as able to serve when small churches become larger.

Small churches deserve to be dealt with in their own right. Denominational programs in education, outreach, and stewardship that are designed for large churches rarely suit the needs of small congrega-

90550

tions. To develop the potential of small congregations, those who lead them and who provide resources for them need to appreciate their potential as small churches.

This series of books is designed specifically for those who lead and support small churches. Each author is someone who cares about and understands the unique possibilities of small congregations.

Several years ago when I began to seek authors to write books in this series, Carl Dudley's name was one of the first to come to mind. Carl's deep concern for small churches and his sensitive understanding of the dynamics of small congregations are equally well known. Perhaps more than anyone else, he has travelled throughout the United States and Canada to inspire and equip leaders of small congregations. I was delighted when he accepted the invitation to write a book in this series.

I was unprepared for his counterproposal: that I join with him as a co-author. He reasoned that our differing experiences coupled with our common concern for small congregations would result in a useful book. As evidenced by the chapters that follow, his argument prevailed. I am honored to be his co-author.

Our choice of title is deliberate and testifies to the central focus of our work. Small congregations have amazing potential. That potential waits to be released by leaders who combine a solid faith in the power of God, a respect for the culture of those among whom they minister, and a clear understanding of the limits and possibilities of the community in which their church finds itself. We believe the strategies leaders choose are most likely to be effective when they fit into the way of life of both congregation and community.

Again and again we have seen small congregations respond to their leaders. When leaders respect them, small congregations develop powerful ministries. This book is based on our experiences as church members, pastors, teachers, and consultants with small congregations that live out such ministries. We want to share our faith in small congregations. We want all those who lead small congregations to discover how to release the potential that waits to be developed where they serve.

**Douglas Alan Walrath**
*Strong, Maine*

# Contents

# Preface

*T*he two of us share so many interests and perspectives that it seemed natural for us to work together on this book. We are both ordained pastors who teach in seminaries. We have studied and written extensively on the small church, and we spend much of our time in the hands-on work of consulting with congregations and church leadership groups. We have been friends for years, worked together in workshops, traded ideas, and focused our attention on the problems and possibilities of small churches in difficult times.

In working together we have also discovered our differences. Our concepts are very similar, but we begin in different places. Our conclusions are often identical, but we have arrived at them by separate routes. Even in our social analysis, one of us always begins with the city and moves toward the rural, and the other begins in the country and moves toward the metropolitan area; in short, we cover the same ground differently. We have learned from each other, and we hope our differences have strengthened the book.

In writing together we reaffirm our convictions that the future of small churches depends upon leaders who can identify and mobilize the strength of the small church "culture" appropriate to the social context and the particular congregation. In chapters 1 and 2, drafted by Doug, we describe the culture of the small church in context, using concepts that liberate church leaders from narrow and negative thinking. In chapters 3 and 4, drafted by Carl, we suggest constructive ways to use and expand the culture of the congregation in such crucial areas as evangelism, stewardship, and social ministry. In the design and preparation of these chapters we have interacted frequently so that the final product is, in essence, our dialogue. We invite others to join our conversation.

**Carl S. Dudley and Douglas Alan Walrath**

# *One*
## CHAPTER

# How Change Is Challenging Small Churches

*T*he theological seminary class is fascinated as they listen to a pastor describe his twelve years of ministry with three small churches. They are moved by his warmth, his genuine concern for those with whom he serves. Participants in the congregations are few in number, but the depth of members' caring for one another is profound. Their worship is vital and engaging. With only minimal facilities and resources at their disposal, children and adults grow in faith. The congregations have been able to accept newcomers to the area as members. Some newcomers have even become leaders alongside local people whose families have been members for generations.

Sensing that the students are taken with the congregations, the pastor cautions, "Your vision for ministry must include more than the church! Pastors who see only the church when they are considering a call overlook as much as they take in. Look at the area. Look at all the possibilities for ministry. Envision yourself and the church in ministry in the area."

The pastor describes the chronic alcoholism that afflicts one quarter of the people who live in the communities and surrounding areas that the three small churches serve—and the churches' ministry among alcoholics. He describes profound poverty and substandard housing—and a housing ministry facilitated by the churches that brings livable housing to more than a dozen families each year. He describes growing unemployment in the shoe and lumbering industries faced by increasing competition from abroad—and the churches' role in beginning a firm that assembles electrical components for computers, a plant that now employs some of the displaced workers.

"These are not typical small churches!" the students protest.

"They were," the pastor responds.

"In the face of social and economic change, most small churches falter. The churches you serve have become more vital. What makes the difference?"

"Faith and the vision you have for the church."

"We know about faith, but what's the vision?"

"The church that is faithful anywhere serves and is composed of who's there."[1]

## Small Congregations: Who's There

The potential of each small congregation is developed through the faith of its participants, the culture(s) they reflect, and the possibilities of the social context in which the church is located. In this book we hope to suggest how small congregations located within various social contexts and shaped by various cultures can develop their potential and live faithfully as churches serving and composed of "who's there."

There is a fundamental interrelationship among social contexts, cultures, and congregations. "Culture" refers to the ways of living that humans impose on the natural environment. A culture includes habits and customs as well as ideas, beliefs, and values. A social context is composed of the social patterns that shape the interrelationships of people, their organizations, and institutions.[2] The particular social patterns that people follow as they live out their everyday lives within a given social context help to shape their culture, to reinforce what they value—what they see as important or essential. The overall dynamic is circu-

    [1]For more information about this ministry see Robert Kimber, "Man with a Mission," *Down East,* vol. 34, no. 5 (December 1987), p. 46.
    [2]H. Richard Niebuhr, *Christ and Culture* (New York: Harper & Row, Publishers, Inc., 1951), chap. 1, section III.

lar: their culture encourages people to live in certain ways; the ways they live shape their culture.

The patterns of life in a congregation are shaped by both the influences of context and the forces of culture. When a social context is stable and integrated, the interrelationship of context, culture, and congregational beliefs is usually harmonious. Social change, however, often undermines and sometimes seriously disrupts this harmony. Such disruptions are especially difficult for small congregations. The dynamics and possibilities of each small church are usually deeply bound up with the context and culture it reflects.

When a social context is challenged by social and economic change, or when persons who represent a different culture move into a social context, the social and cultural connections on which a small church depends—and which its members believe are right—are challenged. It is therefore essential for leaders in a small congregation to understand not only the *specific* patterns that shape small congregations within their particular local social context, but also how social changes may be disrupting or altering the patterns in that context. Both the ways small congregations persist and the ways they are likely to change are shaped by their social contexts.

## Small Churches and Their Social Contexts

There are a wide variety of local social contexts, but most small congregations are located in local contexts within one of three areas: rural, fringe, or city neighborhood. In each of these areas we have identified two local contexts or groups of related local contexts in which small congregations are usually found.

Local social contexts in the rural area include:
- open country and small settlements;
- villages, small towns, and independent cities.

Local social contexts in the fringe area include:
- exurbs where suburban development is just beginning;
- fringe suburbs where suburban development is in full swing.

Local social contexts in city neighborhoods include:
- •ethnic-minority neighborhoods;
- •redeveloping neighborhoods.

Probably the best way to begin to understand how the dynamics of social contexts affect small congregations is to look at the recent history of a small congregation in each area. Then in the next section we will analyze some important contextual patterns and cultural changes that are typical of each context.

## *Rural*

At the turn of the century just over fourteen thousand persons lived in the area around the small town of Matthewstown. Today there are slightly fewer than four thousand inhabitants. In place of the scores of sawmills that furnished lumber to build thousands of homes along the Atlantic seaboard, one largely automated pulp mill remains. The harbor that at one time played host to lumber-carrying ships is now haven only to fishing boats. The once-busy railroad yard is completely gone.

Until six years ago the stately wooden structure of First Church stood amidst the once-elegant homes of the leading citizens of Matthewstown, a physical reminder of the town's golden age. Except during concerts that, thanks to an old endowment, were held twice a year, the six hundred seats in its sanctuary rarely contained more than fifty worshipers. From the Sunday after Christmas until Palm Sunday, the congregation gathered for worship in a chapel area. Heating the large, vaulted sanctuary through the winter was beyond their means. The entire Sunday school could meet in just two classrooms: one for young children and another for the adult class.

Year by year the congregation struggled to maintain the largely unused building. One board member called their financial planning "an exercise in brinkmanship." Frustrated by their inability to attract an ordained minister, they invited an unusually talented student pastor who spent her final year of seminary with them to stay on after her ordination. She did—but not for long. Her suggestions that they abandon the costly building and use their endowment to build a multipurpose, efficient structure more in line with their current needs and means and that they focus some of their energy and resources on social ministries in their community found little support among the members. The longer she stayed, the more they felt she didn't understand them. How could they be First Church without the old building? Of course they would *support* social ministries, but it was difficult for most of them to see themselves directly involved in social ministries. In frustration, the pastor decided they would never change. She moved on.

Recalling the difficulty of attracting an ordained pastor and well aware of the strain paying a fulltime minister had placed on their finances, the congregation agreed to try their regional denominational executive's suggestion that they share a pastor with another church in the village. They decided to try out the arrangement, not out of willingness to work cooperatively with the other church, but because they saw no other way to continue independently.

They had shared the pastor for only six months when tragedy struck—on a cold winter's night the stately building burned. Except for some old record books stored in a fireproof safe, they lost everything. The small congregation with whom they were sharing a pastor immediately invited the congregation of First Church to worship with them, which they were glad to do. It was a surprisingly happy arrangement. For nearly a year the two congregations appeared to be melding into one. Even the choirs merged.

The shared pastor's lack of action during the year that the two congregations worshiped together was intentional. Perhaps if the two congregations spent some time together, he reasoned, they might agree to join together on a permanent basis. When their area denominational executive met with First Church's board to help them begin planning for the future, he suggested just such a marriage. The remaining church building that belonged to the other church was more than adequate for both congregations. In view of First Church's meager resources and the inadequate amount of fire insurance money they had received, why put forth the huge effort it would take to rebuild? Perhaps the fire was a blessing in disguise. Why not simply accept the act of Providence and merge?

The leaders and members of First Church reacted swiftly and firmly. Though the two congregations had shared a single pastor and had worshiped together for nearly a year since the fire, members of First Church would not entertain *any* option for the future that did not include rebuilding. All of the "reasonable" suggestions of the executive came to nought. With no financial help from their denomination, but with solid support from church members and considerable support from many in the community (including members of other churches and even those with no church connection), First Church built a new, traditional, stately, though smaller, building on the site of the one that burned.

### *Fringe*

The members of the congregation in Marksburg were unprepared for change. For 150 years they had simply been "the village church." Now suddenly they found themselves in the midst of an expanding metropolitan area. In the space of only a few years, the church buildings and homes and stores that formed the old village were submerged in a sea of suburban houses, condominiums, apartments, and shopping centers.

A new pastor arrived just as the first of several hundred condominiums were completed. While natives and older newcomers to the area were overwhelmingly opposed to the new developments, the pastor was neither put off nor threatened by the changes. He saw them as a challenge. To him the influx of new persons represented an unprecedented opportunity for the small church.

With great determination and a clear sense of calling, he began to develop a program of ministry designed to reach the new people. Within a few months he was concentrating on ministry to the newcomers. He made scores of calls at their homes. He made changes in the worship service designed to make it more contemporary. He initiated new approaches to Christian education that he felt would upgrade the congregation's offerings in this area and heighten its appeal to the newcomers.

When he made the shift in focus, the pastor was certain the congregation as a whole would support the outreach. He was surprised and openly disappointed when only a few members actually joined in efforts to reach new people. "Evangelism is the heart of the gospel," he emphasized.

His ministry among the newcomers did lead to results. After several months some of them began to participate in the old church. The Sunday school grew in numbers. Contributions increased, relieving a chronic shortage of funds.

For a time, the longstanding members seemed to be pleased. Then the complaints began. The pastor was neglecting visits among the older members. The changes in the worship service brought in unfamiliar language and uncomfortable practices at the expense of favorite hymns and predictable patterns that older members had long found nurturing. New members who made their way into positions of leadership wanted to bring even more change to the church. Much of what they sought both excited and seemed warranted to the pastor.

But increasingly the older leaders began to resist the new direction the church was taking. The new members, supported by the pastor, pushed harder. The crisis came at an annual meeting. The nominating committee, dominated by new members, presented a list of nominees drawn largely from among newcomers. If past patterns at annual meetings had prevailed, the slate would have been adopted unopposed. But the week before the meeting the list of nominees "leaked." A group of concerned older members gathered quietly at one of their homes to prepare an alternate list of nominees. The day prior to the annual meeting, longstanding church members received telephone calls emphasizing the importance of their attendance.

The strategy worked perfectly. When the chairperson of the nominating committee presented her list of nominees, the moderator asked if there were any other nominations. One by one, older members who had been present at the quietly held meeting rose to present alternatives to each committee-endorsed nominee. In every case the alternate was elected.

During the following year the church board, dominated now by old-timers, either questioned or reversed most of the changes of the previous few years. Increasingly discouraged by the well-organized resistance of longstanding members, newcomers began to withdraw from participation. After several confrontations with the board, some of them quite ugly, the pastor accepted a call to another church.

### *City*

Ten years ago when Ann was installed as pastor of St. Luke's church, one of her seminary classmates wondered aloud why someone as exceptional as Ann "had chosen to preside over a church burial."

The situation at St. Luke's church was clearly difficult. The parish had been in the center of racial conflicts that gripped the city during the sixties. In the relative quiet that followed, a succession of pastors did little more than keep it from going under. The church steadily declined in membership. A few years ago it slipped to "mission" status. A majority of the members who still lived in the area now resided in the suburbs.

But Ann was not only committed; she was informed. She was not only prepared to face the reality of St. Luke's present situation, but she had a vision of what the church might be, an informed vision. Before Ann agreed to take on this ministry that her friends advised her against, she spent time visiting and talking with pastors and lay leaders in churches located in neighborhoods similar to the one that surrounded St. Luke's. She looked at churches that were struggling and at some that were thriving. During those visits and conversations she asked herself again and again, *What makes the difference?* And she began to formulate some hunches. She was far from certain about the future when she took on this new ministry, but she had a clear sense of direction.

"If a city church is going to make it, it will have to make it in its neighborhood," one leader in a thriving small congregation in a city neighborhood had told her. Most members of her new congregation were surprised when she used her housing allowance to rent an apartment in a refurbished brownstone one block from St. Luke's. Only later did she—and they—realize how well her instincts had served her.

Her apartment was located where two neighborhood cultures came together. The area to the east toward the river was largely filled with Spanish-speaking persons. To the south, toward St. Luke's church building, the brownstones were being renovated into apartments eagerly sought by the single and married younger adults who worked in the government offices, banks, insurance companies, and as professionals in the city center only six blocks away. Ann got acquainted with her neighbors on *both* sides.

At the same time that she was becoming familiar with the neighborhood, Ann visited every suburban household affiliated with St. Luke's. As she had anticipated, a majority of church officers and board members came from these suburban households. They also accounted for a majority of the inactive members. In the first visit, as she was talking with a member who explained his inattendance by saying St. Luke's had little program to offer that interested him, Ann coined a motto: "Then come down there to invest yourself!" "Invest yourself!" She repeated the motto as she visited and in meetings wherever she came together with people around St. Luke's—and she carefully noted those who were taken with the idea.

Ann began to develop the connections. Some were easier to make than others. A new day-care program quickly filled with children. A "clothes closet" maintained with clothes gathered by some suburban "investors" met real needs among the poorer residents of the neighborhood.

The new urban professionals were more difficult to reach, but the breakthrough idea came in Ann's conversation over coffee with a neighbor in an adjoining brownstone. They decided to try an outreach effort centered on sharing and liturgy. A small group gathered to share their beliefs and to explore believing in a nonjudgmental atmosphere, closing each session with a Communion liturgy.

After her first year in this new parish, Ann shared her experiences with her skeptical seminary classmate. She knew she had hardly begun, but she felt solid. Her classmate was startled to discover she had survived.

## How Contextual Patterns Affect Small Churches

Even when they are immersed in social change and surrounded by newcomers, the longstanding members of locally oriented congregations usually continue to follow old, familiar patterns that are typical of their social context. It is important, therefore, to understand the *specific* patterns that shape small congregations within particular local social contexts and how recent social changes are disrupting these patterns in each context.[3]

Especially in the years since World War II, massive shifts of people and resources have occurred:

- *away from* rural areas, villages, towns and independent cities;
- *out of* inner- and middle-city neighborhoods;
- *into* the suburban fringes of expanding metropolitan regions.

Small congregations rooted in these different contexts are affected differently by the movements of people and resources and by the social, economic, and cultural changes associated with the shifts. Often these changes undermine the traditional pattern of relationship between the local congregation and its local social context. How individual small congregations fare is

[3]For a more complete description of local contexts see Douglas Alan Walrath, "Types of Small Congregations and Their Implications for Planning," in Jackson W. Carroll, ed., *Small Churches Are Beautiful* (New York: Harper & Row, Publishers, Inc., 1977); and Walrath, "Social Change and Local Churches: 1951-75," in Dean R. Hoge and David A. Roozen, eds., *Understanding Church Growth and Decline: 1950–1978* (New York: The Pilgrim Press, 1979).

at least to some extent, usually to a great extent, the result of what happens *to* them as the changes come to their particular local context.

## *Rural Areas and Churches*

Rural areas include:

- open country and settlements of less than 500 persons;
- villages and small towns with 500 to 5,000 persons;
- independent cities with 5,000 to 25,000 persons.

Open country and settlement portions of rural areas are shaped by agriculture, ranching, lumbering, mining, or whatever other land-related industry characterizes the region. Historically, settlements or crossroads contained a school, general store, sometimes a creamery or mill, and a church. In recent years, centralization of services coupled with a loss of population has resulted in the loss of some or all of these businesses and institutions.

Villages and small towns usually grew up as service centers to the surrounding open country. The high school was established here, as was the hospital. Usually physicians and attorneys have their offices here. Some larger villages and small towns serve as the county seat. In each there is a downtown with a business district and one or more banks, and there are several churches.

The independent city is generally based on one industry, often because needed raw material is available from the surrounding countryside. Fabrics, paper, and leather goods are typical products. While the small city has some urban character to it and even includes a variety of ethnic groups in its population, its independent character and small-town flavor mark it as still predominantly rural in culture and attitudes. Churches are spread throughout the independent city—from large (or, as we shall note later, formerly large), downtown churches to small, neighborhood churches that serve distinct denominational and ethnic groups.

The overall pattern of change in nearly all rural areas during the last sixty years is one of loss. The mechanization of agriculture beginning in the early years of this century has steadily and, at times, dramatically resulted in larger and larger farms needing fewer and fewer people to operate them. A similar trend in mining, lumbering, and manufacturing and the increased interconnection of all manufacturing since World War II have resulted in less need for labor in small towns and independent cities. This developing technology and changing economy have encouraged the migration of people from these locales to metropolitan centers where employment opportunities have increased. The few towns and cities that are fortunate enough to have a service industry (such as a college) or a leisure-oriented industry have been least affected by the overall pattern of loss.

As a result of the loss of population and resources, most locales in rural areas have fewer people and are less well-off economically than they were several decades ago. With fewer persons available, community organizations and institutions, including churches, often find they have fewer participants and leaders available to serve their needs. Moreover, the loss is selective. Over the years those best able to move on have done so; persons with better ability who can gain more education are the most likely to leave. As we shall note presently, this selective loss of population hits especially those mainline churches that draw their participants from middle-class and upper middle-class groups.

During the last several decades most mainline congregations located in rural settlements, villages, and small towns have lost members, usually not as a result of weak church programs or pastors, but because so many of those who compose their traditional constituency have moved away. However, compared with congregations located at rural crossroads or in small settlements, small congregations located in rural villages, small towns, and independent cities respond quite differently to the loss.

In villages or small towns, congregations were founded one

by one to minister to particular ethnic or social groups as each settled in and around the town or village. However, as the local population declines and the churches struggle to find enough members to maintain themselves within a reduced pool of potential participants, these historic differences become increasingly blurred. At the same time, most older, small congregations that survive in rural towns, villages, and independent cities traditionally have seen one another as competitors. While cooperative measures, such as sharing pastors or facilities or working together programmatically, seem logical and prudent to incoming pastors and other outsiders, the local churches are often reluctant to adopt them. Not only do the other churches still feel socially and culturally different to them; locals fear that suggesting cooperation is tantamount to admitting to their competitors that their church is weak, and it may encourage the others to compete even more strenuously. So, like the congregation in Matthewstown who put forth great effort to rebuild their church, village and town congregations especially seek to preserve their independence—even at great cost.

Rarely are similar feelings of competition a controlling factor among the members of rural congregations located at crossroads or in small settlements where they have always been the only church. In fact, many of these congregations have functioned within cooperative arrangements for some time. They likely do not experience cooperation competitively for three reasons. (1) Those who make their living from the land have a long history of cooperation (sharing machinery, joining together at threshing time and for barn raisings, and so forth). (2) The churches with which they cooperate do not feel like competitors because they are some distance away. They are not seen as competitors because they are literally not in sight. (3) Rural churches, despite the differences among them, are often more similar in attitudes, culture, and faith than churches in metropolitan areas.

Crossroads or small-settlement congregations are also usually more accustomed than village congregations to making do with what they have. They have lived with reduced resources and fewer participants for many years. Most have long accepted (perhaps reluctantly) the need to share a pastor with other congregations or to be served by a pastor who is only part-time. Crossroads congregations are more likely to be concerned with survival per se than with being better than others.

## Fringe Areas and Churches

When a metropolitan area expands, it overruns the open country, villages, and towns of the rural area that surrounds it. Locales in the early stages of that overrunning are termed "exurban"; those in the middle and later stages are called "suburban." The village of Marksburg which we described in the opening pages of this chapter is located in an exurban area that is now becoming suburban.

In the exurban or early stages of metropolitan development, those who move into the area generally seek and affirm the rural lifeways (a way or manner of living, especially associated with an occupation or location) that characterize the area. These newcomers are usually either affluent persons who can afford high-cost housing on large lots or commuters who are willing to pay the price of long-distance commuting in exchange for the greater physical space, psychic freedom, and lower-cost housing that is still available some distance from the metropolitan center.

When suburban development reaches an exurban area, the early newcomers and locals often join forces (as they did in Marksburg) to resist the suburban development. They see the rapid growth in people and housing and the large shopping centers and industrial parks as a threat to the way of life they value. However, they usually lose the battle. The newcomers are not only generally more affluent, educated, aggressive, and articulate, but they also arrive in large numbers. Political and industrial forces that bring the newcomers to the formerly rural area are overwhelming. As the suburban development proceeds, people and institutions that represent the old way of life are either transformed or isolated. Small congregations that remain in the suburban, formerly rural areas often seem like culturally contained institutions serving those few who still affirm a culture and way of life that used to be.

When those who hold one set of values and live according to patterns that stem from and reinforce these values move into an area occupied by persons whose life patterns stem from and reinforce another set of values, conflicts are likely to emerge. The natives and early newcomers in the suburb-ringed, formerly rural village of Marksburg are committed to a way of life that is rooted in the social context of traditional village life. That local social context provides the patterns they value and honor in their daily lives, including the ways they relate to the church, the position the church occupies, and the roles the church plays in their lives.

The newcomers, by contrast, do not experience the shaping forces of these particular local roots. Most of them live more regionally than locally. To say it another way: The region is their locale. Most of them reside in one place, work in another, attend church in yet another, shop in other places, seek recreation in others, and so on. The different aspects of their living are not likely to occur in one place, nor are they likely to feel (as most of the villagers do) that their lives would be better if most or all of these different aspects could be brought together and occur in the same space.

As a group the newcomers are not as likely as the villagers to place a consistently higher value on one particular place or aspect of their lives (like home or church). Nor are they as likely to want to be found consistently in certain places at certain times. In other words, they are as likely to go out to dinner and a movie after work as to go home. They are as likely to want to go skiing for the weekend as to want to be at home. They feel equally at home in several aspects (places) of their lives.

Natives, on the other hand, are more likely to live out many, if not most, aspects of their lives in the same place or space. They are more likely to work locally, shop locally, and play locally. And they typically carry on many or all aspects of their living with the same people. Locals who live with the same people in many, if not most, aspects of their lives tend to experience relationships and institutions pervasively and wholistically. Even natives who choose or are forced to carry on some functions away from the village usually continue to experience the village locale as primary and central. Thus, a local who must commute to work every day does so only out of necessity and stays away only so long as necessary. The goal is to be home (in the village), because home is where one can truly "be."[4]

Natives also experience church as desirably and properly local. They see their congregation as a church of the place, of the locale. As such they continue a historic perspective and traditional way of life into the present. Historically many, if not most, small churches have been identified with the places to which they belong. Most natives hold fast to that historic identity even in the face of drastic social changes and large influxes of newcomers.

For example, the Presbyterian church in Maine where I (DAW) am active is known locally as the Fairbanks church. Though the village of Fairbanks was integrated into the surrounding town many years ago and thus disappeared as an actual entity, the church is still identified as the Fairbanks church. Though the congregation changed their denominational affiliation more than three decades ago, among the natives who compose the majority of members, the church is never referred to as the "Presbyterian" church. Despite all the changes, it still remains the church of the place.

Those of us who have our roots in suburban areas or who take our cultural values from the fast-paced, technological, media-dominated, global, mass culture are often unaware of the degree to which most small congregations reflect a traditional, local culture. Both the pastor and the suburban newcomers to

[4]For a more complete discussion of these different perspectives see Douglas Alan Walrath, *Frameworks: Patterns of Living and Believing Today* (New York: The Pilgrim Press, 1987), ch. 2. See also Robert K. Merton, *Social Theory and Social Structure,* enlarged ed., (New York: The Free Press, 1968), and Wade Clark Roof, *Community and Commitment: Religious Plausibility in a Liberal Protestant Church* (New York: Elsevier Science Publishing Co., Inc., 1978).

the congregation in Marksburg are "from away" (to use a term Mainers apply indiscriminantly to anyone who is not a local person). Their lifeways, values, dreams, needs, and visions differ substantially from those held by local persons who have been members of that small church for most of their lives.

Unwittingly the new pastor in Marksburg reflects only the culture of the latest newcomers as he defines the shape the congregation should take to fulfill its proper mission. The larger scale, faster pace, and greater diversity he envisions for the congregation fit the culture of these newcomers—which happens to be his culture as well. To serve his and the newcomers' needs adequately the congregation will become larger and pluralistic, diversify its program, expand its organization to support that program, and concentrate on contemporary concerns and societal issues.

These proposed changes do not feel like progress to the locals. They balk at the developments suggested by the pastor and newcomers. Most of the locals see the proposed changes as a challenge to their entire way of life. Although they usually embrace a variety of personalities among their members, most small village churches relate primarily to the culture of a well-defined social group within the local community. The influx of new members and diversity of program threaten the stable, cohesive relationships that provide secure places and clear roles for the older members. The novelty the pastor introduces to appeal to newcomers undermines the predictable routine within worship services that nurtures the old-timers. The longstanding members are drawn to this church not because it facilitates change, but because it provides welcome stability in the midst of unwelcome change. In fact, from the perspective of some locals, even those newcomers who join the church continue to feel like outsiders in the congregation. Their different attitudes and priorities and mobile way of life show that they do not completely belong.

To many of the old-timers the newcomers do not seem stable enough to be entrusted with the overall direction of the church. When the nominating committee proposes a slate dominated by newcomers, the natives realize that the changes the newcomers want could become reality. The old-timers reassert their power. They block the newcomers from positions of leadership because they believe the newcomers' values and behavior demonstrate that they do not appreciate the time-tested, essential values that have always stood at the center of the church's life. Until they can appreciate these values, they should not be given positions of power.

Of course, the newcomers are being faithful to *their* culture. Even those who do join the village church do not expect (nor would most of them want) to adapt completely to the local culture. They neither want nor expect to invest themselves *to belong forever* either to the local church or to the local culture. Most newcomers who join the church join for specific purposes, not to indicate an overall or lasting commitment to this congregation and community. They are more likely to participate only in specific programs that meet their needs or relate to their concerns. Most of them know that sooner or later they are likely to move on. Neither the village nor the local culture nor the local congregation call forth permanent commitments from them. Their primary commitments and concerns range over a much larger arena than this village.

The widespread belief that a large influx of population means more people are "available" to a fringe small church is generally misleading. Persons who relocate from city neighborhoods or rural areas to suburbia usually move culturally as well as geographically. They *become* suburban. They themselves change in the process of relocating. By the time they arrive in the suburban area they have *become* suburban. They now represent a culture quite different from the culture they left behind. Their living ranges across many miles and involves them with various groups of people. Instead of being persons who expect to invest themselves and concentrate their living and affection in a local context and congregation, they are oriented to a larger social context that is regional, even national. Even those among them who join existing small congregations usually do not turn out to be the kind of new members locals hoped they would be.

Like the fringe congregation in Marksburg, many small churches located in rural areas that become suburban are unable (and sometimes unwilling) to make the changes needed to attract and include such transformed constituents. Longstanding residents usually continue to perceive the church within a rural or village framework. Like those who lead rural congregations in areas of declining population and those who lead city-neighborhood congregations, nothing in their history has prepared them for the challenges they now face.

## City Neighborhoods and Churches

In the city, small churches are most likely to be found in inner-city and inner-urban neighborhoods, with a few small churches in outer-urban neighborhoods.[5] Inner-city neighborhoods are the traditional areas of "first settlement" that have played host to successive waves of immigrants over the years. Most were originally located next to warehouse districts or heavy industry. Residences, largely multifamily, are mixed in with with businesses and stores. These neighborhoods often serve as residential areas for the city's poor.

Inner-urban neighborhoods are the traditional working-class neighborhoods of the city, composed originally of two-family and some single-family homes gathered about businesses and stores. As successive waves of immigrants improved themselves, many have been able to move into working-class, inner-urban neighborhoods. Today, alongside of whatever group dominates, many of these neighborhoods have a few remaining inhabitants who represent each of the various groups that have moved into them over the years.

Outer-urban neighborhoods are the most affluent areas of the city, composed largely of single-family homes and well-defined, concentrated business and shopping districts. In many cities these neighborhoods continue to be prime residential locations.

More recently some neighborhoods near the city center have

[5]For a more complete discussion of these types, see Walrath, *Frameworks: Patterns of Living and Believing Today.*

become attractive residential locations for younger, urban professionals. This new wave of urban immigrants seek sound residences they can redevelop. As they upgrade the housing, it often moves beyond the means of those who are poor, who are then forced to move elsewhere in search of affordable housing.

As successive groups of newcomers moved into the city, they founded churches within their own cultures and traditions, many of which now survive as smaller congregations than the original one. Especially in the years following World War II, as more and more members of these congregations became middle class and were able to move to the suburbs, many city congregations lost members. Members of other ethnic groups who moved into the neighborhood were not attracted by the existing churches. The churches were not of their culture. As a result, many small congregations in city neighborhoods are remnants of much larger congregations, possessed of buildings that are expensive to maintain and well beyond their needs. The typical small church in the city is usually a smaller church, and many are quite dependent economically and for leadership on the continued loyalty of suburban members who formerly lived in the neighborhood.

In city neighborhoods social change also challenges the historical patterns of relationship between church and context. Like those who have spent their lives in rural areas, longstanding residents of city neighborhoods see their church as deeply intertwined with its local context. Like many rural pastors, their pastors have long responded to the needs of residents of the neighborhood, regardless of whether the residents are actually members. However, as their traditional constituencies have moved away, city churches have not only lost participants, but many now find that a large proportion of their members are commuters.

The typical city-neighborhood church's core dilemma is often reflected in the members' chronic complaints about the lack of adequate parking. In pre-World War II days such a lack of parking spaces was rarely a problem. Most of the members lived in the neighborhood within walking distance of the church building. But the increasing affluence of the post-World War II generation of church members, combined with changes in the composition of the church's neighborhood, often encourages many church families to move out of the neighborhood. Those relocated members who continue to be active now commute to the neighborhood church for worship and meetings and are frustrated by the lack of parking spaces.

Many of these commuter members lose touch with the church's immediate neighborhood. Several years ago I worked with one such city-neighborhood church, an old German Reformed church, still composed largely of those with German roots. The congregation numbers less than one hundred members. Most of the remaining members now reside some distance from the church building; only about 15 percent are residents of the neighborhood around the church building. The bulk of the active congregation are commuter members.

Over the past two decades more and more Hispanics have moved into the church's neighborhood. The longstanding members, especially the commuters, have made little contact with these Spanish-speaking newcomers. In conversations with church members it became clear that the pastor (a man in his early sixties) and consistory were frightened by the newcomers. Neither church members nor pastor knew how to reach out to those around them. Nothing in their history or experience up to now had prepared them or encouraged them to reach beyond their own cultural limits. Like most small churches, they had always been able to continue and had expected to continue by serving their own kind.

The geographical distance that separates many of the active members of this city congregation from the immediate neighborhood around their church building aggravates the cultural distance they feel between themselves and the new persons who have moved into that neighborhood. They lack opportunities to build personal relationships that persons from different social and cultural groups often form when they share the same neighborhood. Such personal relationships can break down biases, relieve anxiety, and lead to cultural understanding.

When those who lead a city church are largely nonresidents of its neighborhood, there are few natural encounters between them and the neighborhood residents. They then have to create opportunities to gain the understanding they need to build bridges between themselves and those who now live in the church's neighborhood. Creating such opportunities takes considerable effort, yet doing so is absolutely necessary. The future of the small church in a city neighborhood depends on its ability to become a significant factor in the lives of those who now live in its immediate neighborhood.

## Summary

In this chapter we have described the impact of social and economic change on small congregations. We have considered the effects of those changes on congregations in three kinds of areas—rural, fringe, and city—and in local social contexts within those areas.

We have discussed changes affecting rural congregations located in open country, small settlements, villages, small towns, and independent cities. Social and economic losses continue to have profound effects on many congregations in these areas.

We have seen that congregations located in former rural crossroads and villages now at the fringes of metropolitan regions often experience a collision of cultures.

We have noted how shifting populations in cities and neighborhood changes are reflected in emerging ethnic-minority congregations, declining neighborhood churches, and redeveloping congregations.

We have identified how their history, tradition, and past experience shape the ways small congregations in various social contexts respond to the challenges of change.

Those who responsibly lead small congregations recognize that congregation, culture, and context function as a unit. To recall the vision of the pastor serving the three-church parish, a faithful congregation serve and are composed of "who's there" where they are now.

In the next chapter we will examine how the various images that congregations hold of themselves and of the kind(s) of people to whom they can relate define and limit what they will attempt. In the same way that we must accept the limits of our social context to discover possible ministries, we must also discern the potential of the particular church we seek to lead. And churches are as particular as contexts.

## Questions for Discussion and Reflection

These questions are directed not only to local leaders in small churches, but also to regional and national leaders who can apply them on a denominational level.

1a. Which of the following best describes our social context?
   • Rural crossroads or settlement
   • Rural village, small town, or independent city
   • Former rural area becoming exurban or suburban
   • City neighborhood

1b. How are changes that have or are occurring in our social context affecting our church?

2. In what ways are the active members of our congregation socially and culturally distinctive? Are we similar or different from most of those who live around our church building? from those who are new to our area, or who have become the majority in our area?

3. As we think about developments in our social context, what challenges do they represent for our congregation? Which of these are most important for us to address immediately?

4. As we think of various possibilities for our church, what are some options our church members are likely to support?

# *Two*
## CHAPTER

# Discovering
# the Connections

*T*he newly appointed evangelism committee of First Church in Matthewstown was frustrated. Except for a brief surge in the 1950s, for nearly five decades the total membership of First Church had become smaller. Committee members reminisced about the days of their own youth when nearly twice as many people attended worship and more than six times as many children attended Sunday school. This decline in participants by itself was painful enough to watch, but the startling growth of a new Independent Bible Church just outside the village aggravated their frustration. The Bible Church's new building, its young families, and dozens of children offered a challenging contrast to First Church's handful of children, mostly gray-haired worshipers, and many empty pews.

For an hour and a half committee members talked about the "reasons" for the differences between themselves and the other church. First Church's Sunday school teachers weren't committed enough. Parents didn't see to it that their children attended like parents used to do years ago. Their minister's sermons weren't biblical enough, and she didn't make enough visits. The discussion ended with a unanimous conclusion. First Church needed to get back to basics: to good, old-fashioned, Bible-based religion. Then they would thrive again, like the growing Bible Church.

Yet in spite of their strong words, committee members knew that they and the rest of the congregation of First Church would not put forth the effort needed to make the changes. Though they couldn't envision another course of action, they knew their church could not become like that Bible Church. While they envied the Bible Church's dynamic growth, they knew they didn't have the heart to emulate that Bible Church. And try as they might, they sensed that even a sustained effort on their church's part would not change its overall image in the eyes of the community. Even a significant outreach effort would not convince the community that First Church was or ever could be like that Independent Bible Church.[1]

Why did the evangelism committee of First Church feel so pessimistic about the possibility of changing their image? What kinds of powerful and lasting impressions do churches make? How do the reputations they establish determine who wants and feels able to participate in which church? What shapes the kinds of connections congregations can make with people in their contexts?

## Social Position

In the early 1970s I began to categorize small congregations according to the reputations or "social positions" they have gained in the communities or neighborhoods they serve.[2] The ways churches connect to their social contexts are determined by the social positions in which they become established. Both consciously and unconsciously members of a community or neighborhood do or do not identify themselves with a particular congregation on the basis of their sense of the social position

[1]An earlier version of some of the material in this chapter appeared as a research report by Douglas Alan Walrath and Sherry Walrath in *The Open Door* (Spring 1988), published by Bangor Theological Seminary. This research was conducted under the auspices of the Small Church Leadership Program at Bangor Theological Seminary, with the support of the Lilly Endowment.

[2]See Douglas Alan Walrath, "Types of Small Congregations and Their Implications for Planning," in Jackson W. Carroll, ed., *Small Churches Are Beautiful* (New York: Harper & Row, Publishers, Inc., 1977); and Walrath, "Social Change and Local Churches: 1951-75," in Dean R. Hoge and David A. Roozen, eds., *Understanding Church Growth and Decline*: 1950–1978 (New York: The Pilgrim Press, 1979).

that congregation holds. In other words, people decide whether a particular church can be "their" church on the basis of the way it appears to them and to others.

Congregations usually become established in one of three social positions: Dominant, Denominational, or Distinctive.

*The Dominant congregation* is "the" church in its neighborhood or community—the "tall-steeple" church. Local residents usually see it as a moneyed, prestigious church. Often the church building is located on the town square or on a corner lot. Its members expect the best in pastoral leadership and program. People who count (or who want to count) belong to this church. It appears (and most of its members are seen as) socially dominant.

Dominant churches usually thrive when there is an ample supply of relatively affluent, middle-class persons who support the superior leadership, program, and facilities typical of a Dominant congregation. Wherever such a constituency declines, as it has in many rural communities and small towns and city neighborhoods, Dominant churches also tend to decline. The economic declines in many rural areas and cities that have encouraged middle-class persons to move elsewhere have had a great impact on Dominant churches.

The actual losses, however, often do not lead immediately to changed perceptions either on the part of members or those who live in the neighborhood around a Dominant church. Even when they lose their constituency, most Dominant churches do not simultaneously lose their local image. Despite actual losses of members and economic support, they are still viewed locally as "the" church. As a result, those who remain in the community who are not the traditional constituency of the Dominant church still do not see it as accessible to them.

Many pastors and lay leaders of declining Dominant churches do not seem to appreciate how long a Dominant church continues to be identified with its traditional image— even when it is no longer powerful. They wonder why so few persons in the community respond even to concentrated efforts to welcome them or to develop programs that meet their needs and interests. Usually such efforts will not bear fruit until those toward whom they are directed are able to change their image of the Dominant church, that is, until they can conceive of the Dominant church as their church. Even people who participate in church programs and who benefit from the church's ministry will not be able to see themselves as members. They will usually not become regular participants or members until the church gains a new and broader reputation. Often a Dominant church needs to persist for many years in efforts designed to broaden its appeal before others in its area begin to see it as a church in which they can participate.

*The Denominational congregation* is defined locally by the denominational label it carries. People who belong to a Denominational church are identified locally as "Methodists" or "Presbyterians" or "Baptists," in other words, by the denominational label attached to the local church. Long-standing residents, as well as newcomers who have roots in a given denomination and who continue to function as church members on the basis of these roots, comprise a Denominational congregation.

Members of Denominational small congregations are often very loyal to their church. Those who possess such a strong sense of denominational loyalty will maintain their ties to a Denominational church even during periods when they are dissatisfied with a particular minister and/or church program. Some members may drop out or withhold their contributions when they are dissatisfied; they may even attend another church for a time. But they rarely withdraw their membership. Their sense of identity both with the congregation and the denomination beyond the local congregation encourages them to wait for a change of pastor or program. When such a change occurs, they usually return.

A Denominational church thrives so long as there is an adequate supply of persons who want to be identified with a congregation connected to the denomination it represents. Like the Dominant church, when its traditional supporters move away and the Denominational church is still seen denominationally, it usually declines. Currently in many rural communities and city neighborhoods, small congregations affiliated with denominations that are seen as middle-class have declined. Middle-class persons and their grown children who have always provided the core of the Denominational church's participants have moved away. But the church still retains the same image; it still appears to be their church.

The specific reputation, polity, and policies of its denomination can help or hinder the local congregation that is clearly identified with a particular denomination. For example, a denomination that can provide uninterrupted pastoral leadership for its small churches through appointments or one that moves quickly to provide solid support for congregations seeking new pastors may strengthen the position of its congregations. The position of a Denominational congregation in the community can also be strengthened or weakened by what local leaders say about their experience with the denomination or by what local people see and hear about the denomination in the media. Pastors report local leaders are most frustrated when they are called upon to defend locally unpopular positions their denomination takes on national issues on the one hand, while receiving little support or recognition for their efforts to keep their small church going on the other.

*The Distinctive congregation* is known for one, and occasionally more than one, emphasis. While it may embrace a typical variety of church functions within its life, it is best known locally for its emphasis. Sometimes people type the Distinctive congregation according to a theological emphasis ("fundamental," "liberal"). Sometimes its worship style ("charismatic") sets it apart. In other instances residents see its clearly local control and lack of denominational entanglements ("independent") as its major attraction. Other Distinctive congregations are identified by their program focus (the "social action" church, the church with the "healing ministry").

People who want to participate in and/or be identified with the emphasis of the Distinctive congregation are drawn to it, often from a wide area. As a result, Distinctive congregations stand or fall almost entirely on their local appeal. Most are neither aided nor hindered by a denominational connection—if they happen to have one. Because they highlight local characteristics, whatever locally distinguishes the Distinctive congregation governs the appeal it holds for those in its area. When whatever it represents is appealing, the Distinctive church thrives; when its focus is not sufficiently engaging to enough people in its area, the Distinctive church suffers.

Small Distinctive congregations that are growing currently include congregations identified with theological and social positions that are popular among those who now live in many city neighborhoods and rural areas, including churches that characterize themselves as "fundamental," "pentecostal," or "independent." In fact, in many city neighborhoods and rural areas, newly established Distinctive congregations centered on popular values are growing in the face of declining Denominational and Dominant congregations. Many pastors and lay leaders in mainline congregations are frustrated by their inability to bridge the reputational gap between the Dominant and Denominational congregations they serve and the people who now surround them.

In some cases, the obvious denominational connection of Denominational and many Dominant congregations and their pastors seems to be a liability. There is a significant culture gap between many rural residents and the direction mainstream denominations often take. The pastor who now serves a mainstream congregation in these locations is sometimes caught in the tension between the local culture in which he or she serves and the denomination with which he or she is affiliated. The core question such pastors face is how to help their Dominant or Denominational small congregation widen its appeal to include persons who currently are not attracted to their, or any, congregation, while retaining their own and their congregation's theological integrity and relationship to the larger church and world. In other words, how can a pastor straddle with integrity the cultures—social and theological, historical and contemporary—within and around a small congregation? That core question will increasingly become the focus of this book.

## Cultural Appeal

What we call "cultural appeal" is a second factor that shapes the way small congregations relate to their social contexts. Data from a recent study of small rural congregations in northern New England indicate clearly that the cultural appeal that congregations hold—and encourage—shapes them.[3] Pastors and other leaders interviewed in the study described small congregations in terms of three kinds of cultural appeal: "newcomer" congregations, "indigenous" congregations, and "culturally mixed" congregations. These categories describe congregations in other parts of the country as well.

Predictably, *newcomer congregations* are most often located in communities or neighborhoods where the population is increasing, either on the edge of an expanding metropolitan region or in redeveloping city neighborhoods. Newcomer congregations, as the name suggests, are dominated by persons who are relatively new to the areas the congregations serve.

Newcomer congregations on the edges of expanding metropolitan regions seem to be attracting new members from among those who are moving into these formerly rural areas precisely because the churches still *appear* to be rural and small. These small churches embody the traditional culture many newcomers want to be part of when they move to the kind of area these churches serve. Demographically, newcomers to these areas tend to be either older middle-aged persons beginning or about to begin retirement, or younger middle-aged persons, usually married and with children. An area's relative proximity to a metropolitan hub determines which one of the two groups will be in the majority in a specific locale. Areas farther away tend to attract older middle-aged persons or retirees and to be more leisure oriented. Those closer to the metropolitan hub tend to attract younger middle-aged persons who need a closer proxim-

[3]See Sherry Walrath and Douglas Alan Walrath, *The Open Door.*

ity to places of employment. Regardless of their age group, newcomers usually move to the fringe area to gain the benefits of rural living. They see the small church within their vision (and understanding) of rural culture. However, when we listen to pastors and lay leaders from these newcomer churches talk about their congregations, the lifeway they describe seems to reflect mainstream, metropolitan, urban U.S. culture as much as it does rural culture.

Though leaders in most newcomer congregations are still drawn both from among newcomers and those who are native to the area the church serves, in a majority of newcomer congregations the newcomers have more influence on the direction the church is taking. Perhaps newcomers have begun to dominate the leadership in these congregations because newcomers tend to have more years of formal education, are more articulate, and usually are younger than natives. Whatever the source of the newcomers' dominance, it often lifts newcomer congregations from their cultural roots. Those indigenous residents who still participate in newcomer congregations are more likely than other natives to have adopted some of the attitudes and values of mainstream society.

Once the connection with traditional local culture is strained in a congregation, those who are native to its area and who still reflect traditional culture are less likely to be active. Many local persons do not feel comfortable in newcomer congregations that reflect the urban culture of non-natives. Some of these alienated locals become active in Distinctive congregations; others drop out of church participation entirely. In fact some of the growth of Distinctive, independent, fundamentalist churches in rural areas may be occurring as a result of the waning appeal of mainline churches to local natives.

Most seminary-educated ministers, especially those with suburban roots, find newcomer congregations the easiest "rural" small churches to serve. While the newcomer church appears to be rural, the members (and especially the leaders) reflect many of the values of the larger culture within which the minister was educated and with which he or she still identifies. The church is closer to the culture from which such ministers come than it is to the traditional local culture that surrounds it.

Newcomer congregations in redeveloping city neighborhoods reflect a similar collision of cultures. Many are older Dominant and Denominational churches now gaining members from among newly arrived middle-class neighborhood residents who have chosen to live in the city to gain the benefits of urban culture. Some of these newcomers have moved to the city to express their social concern as well. They are committed to making the city a better place for all persons to live, and they see the church as a vehicle to express their social commitment. Yet, committed as they are, often their social position and culture are alien to those who may make up the majority of persons in the neighborhood the church serves. Actually these current new arrivals are socially and culturally closer to those who participated in many city neighborhood churches a generation or two ago. However, their middle-class status and lifeway place them far away culturally from neighborhood persons, especially ethnic minorities, who may have begun to participate in the city congregation during the last two decades.

*Indigenous* churches lie at the opposite end of the cultural appeal spectrum. As the name suggests, the majority of members active in indigenous churches are native to the area or neighborhood the church serves.

Members of rural indigenous churches usually represent the established families in their area. Their roots often go back three or more generations, and, of course, nearly all the members of each extended family are members of the same indigenous church. It is not uncommon for members of one or two extended families to dominate the life of a small indigenous congregation.

Rural indigenous churches tend to be located in areas that are farthest away from any metropolitan area. In fact, mainline small churches in these areas are almost always indigenous churches. Such churches are not only small, but considerably smaller than they were several decades ago. These congregations are the least likely churches in their area to replenish aging members through natural increase. Largely composed as they are of middle-class members, their children most often leave the community to seek higher education and employment —and never return. Their location in a depopulated area, coupled with their local, reputational identity as Dominant or Denominational churches, has brought many mainline indigenous churches to a state of crisis. How long can our church continue when most of the members are now too old to produce more descendants? is a recurrent question one hears in such congregations.

Rural, mainline, indigenous small churches that have traditionally been composed of middle-class members rarely benefit from newcomers, because immigrants to their communities usually are not middle-class, either in attitude or economically. In fact, such newcomers (sometimes called "refugees from the sixties") are likely to be repelled by the mainline churches' apparent connection to the larger society which these newcomers want to leave behind. Eroded as they are, many mainline indigenous congregations today are older, smaller, weakened churches whose members are anxious and resentful in the face of change. They may feel isolated from the denomination and not consider it as a source of help.

Rural Distinctive indigenous churches that are not affiliated with any mainline denomination are often the most recently established churches in their areas. A large number of these congregations have emerged in recent years among persons who have chosen to remain in rural areas and to stand apart culturally from the dominant urban, American mainstream culture. Such persons represent a non-middle-class subculture, distinctive in character, like an ethnic-minority subculture. Their often fundamentalist or pentecostal theology and style of worship highlight their distinctiveness. They rarely relate to or include those who are not within the cultural group they serve. Yet, even with their exclusiveness (or, as some believe, because of their exclusiveness) many of these churches are thriving. The relatively higher birthrate and younger age of their members and their cultural appeal to many of those who now live in rural areas have placed these indigenous congregations in the majority in many rural areas. In many locales they have more participants than the established, mainline churches.

Many pastors and denominational officials seem frustrated in their efforts to understand and help indigenous small churches. Such congregations *are* difficult churches for pastors to serve unless they also are indigenous. The "outsider" pastor finds few with whom to identify either within the congregation or the community at large. Pastors of these congregations often describe themselves (and their families) as excruciatingly lonely. They don't fit locally, and most denominations do not know how to support them.

In between newcomer and indigenous congregations are a group of churches we call *"culturally mixed"* to indicate that they include both indigenous persons and newcomers. Most small churches that continue as culturally mixed congregations for more than a few years are located in city neighborhoods. The cultural mixing of locals and newcomers in congregations located in those exurban fringe areas where a metropolitan region is just beginning to overrun a formerly rural area is usually both stressful and temporary.

Newcomers to an exurban fringe area (like Marksburg, to which we referred in the last chapter) are usually persons who want the best of two worlds. They want the cultural and economic benefits of metropolitan society along with the space ("psychic breathing space," as one person termed it) and freedom of rural life. These long-distance commuters who move into the fringe area that lies between the truly suburban and truly rural are more likely than true suburbanites to carry negative feelings about urban society. Many newcomers to the fringe area have intentionally left the urban society and its lifeways behind (at least so they believe) to embrace a rural lifeway. They willingly travel long distances to their places of employment and adapt their lives to exist on somewhat less income (for example, cut wood with which to heat) in order to be able to live as much as possible out of the urban "rat race."

But these newcomers differ from those who choose to live in

truly rural areas. While both groups agree in their pursuit of a simpler lifeway, those who immigrate to fringe areas want simplicity *combined with a middle-class level of affluence.* They want to live in a rural location that permits them to commute to work that pays well and that is close to a metropolitan center to which they can travel to enjoy the cultural benefits of urban living. They want the best of both worlds.

When these fringe newcomers become active in local churches alongside those who are native to the area, the churches become what we call culturally mixed congregations. Such newcomers usually try to carry their dual lifeway into the church. They want the congregation to represent the best of both worlds. They want a church that combines traditional rural folksiness with an up-to-date educational program, for example.

While local persons may welcome these newcomers at first, if the newcomers push for too much change (in other words, for more change than the locals want), the culturally mixed congregation becomes a stressful congregation. Such congregations face real hazards. Those in which newcomers truly dominate often discover they are losing their appeal to long-standing residents. For example, denominationally affiliated churches in formerly rural areas that have a significant number of active newcomers are especially prone to being perceived as local representatives of denominations that are rooted in what many locals see as an alien larger culture. When such culturally mixed congregations lose their appeal to those who are native to the area and are unable to broaden their appeal sufficiently to include a large number of new persons moving into the area, they can lose heavily. They end up as churches that appeal to *neither* locals nor newcomers.

Interestingly, the tension between locals and newcomers is sometimes resolved when the locals discover that the newcomers came to the fringe area precisely because they share the locals' critical attitude toward the larger society and its institutions. In such instances newcomers and locals find a common cause: they join together to resist the larger world in general.

They oppose the continuing suburban development of their area and denominational policies and programs that they associate with the larger urban culture.

While the kinds of persons they include may be different, culturally mixed small congregations in city neighborhoods face similar dynamics and dilemmas. When longstanding members, especially older longstanding members of a traditional mainline church seek to include ethnic-minority persons or newly arrived younger adults who are intent on redeveloping a city neighborhood, they also may face a clash of cultures within. The tensions here may be even more difficult to resolve than those in culturally mixed fringe congregations. Ethnic-minority members in city neighborhoods may feel that upwardly mobile younger adults are crowding them out of both the congregation and neighborhood. And they may be right.

Ministers who serve culturally mixed congregations often describe them as among the most difficult to pastor. Some of these pastors feel stressed between the culture of those who are native to the area and the more cosmopolitan culture of the denominations to which they are attached. They describe themselves as torn between the desire to adapt their ministry to the needs and culture of the congregations they serve and the realization that such a commitment may alienate them from their denominational ethos. When they have lived for a time in a fringe area or city neighborhood, some pastors even become ambivalent about the culture they want to belong to. These pastors want to minister within the culture of those who now compose the neighborhood and, at the same time, hold on to nurturing elements and relationships within their own culture. We shall have suggestions for those who seek to function in such a bridging ministry in the final chapters of this book.

Finally, stressed as they are between two cultures and sometimes eroded of resources and leadership, culturally mixed congregations are especially vulnerable to conflict. Ministers who serve in these congregations are painfully aware of their need for conflict-management skills.

To summarize: A small congregation's identity as Dominant,

Denominational, or Distinctive, and the composition of its group of leaders (newcomers or locals or a mixture of the two) determine the kinds of persons who are likely to feel that this church can be their church. Once congregations are clearly identified in their areas, changes in social position and cultural appeal are very difficult to establish.

## Seeking Possibilities Within Change

Leaders in most small congregations are not accustomed to looking beyond their congregation and culture either to understand why their church is changing or to define options. Historically, any difficulties a congregation may have encountered were usually caused by internal factors such as poor program or inadequate leadership. Now the difficulties the congregation is experiencing are being caused by changes that are happening "to" it; the problems originate not within the church, but from without.

In the past, leaders who tried to steer a small congregation away from its history or tradition usually misguided it. The social boundaries that separated the constituencies of various congregations have always been very clear. In fact, often the lines were so well established that local leaders who lived most of their lives in a locale assumed their church would always have to live within its established social boundaries, even in the face of great change. Most likely it is difficult for these leaders to look beyond their tradition for options because small churches in their local context have always had a well-defined, rigid, social and cultural identity.

Social change brings unprecedented challenge to many leaders in small congregations. The decline in the number of persons who have always supported a small church, perhaps coupled with the arrival of persons who are not attracted to that church, means that the culture the congregation understands and can relate to is declining, even disappearing. The church may be surrounded by persons whose culture and way of life are alien, and at times, even seem threatening. Under these circumstances the church finds itself in a vastly different social context. The old explanations don't explain any more. The old, reliable approaches to problems fail.

Yet even in the midst of such change and frustration, it is hard to try new approaches. Leaders still feel the power of the old categories. Both of us can recall attempts to encourage congregations to reach beyond their social boundaries. I (DAW) remember well my first effort:

During my ministry with a small congregation in a New York village, I found that many of those with whom I had developed deep, pastoral relationships would not participate in my congregation. Only later did I see a systematic pattern to their refusal. That congregation is the prestige (Dominant) church of the village. Old established families, professionals, and new arrivals who hold prominent positions or own major businesses in the village are seen as the kind of people who go to that church. Other congregations in the village are seen variously as the teachers' and small-business owners' church (Denominational—United Methodist), the farmers' and workers' church (Denominational—Lutheran), the church that serves the best of those who live on "the wrong side of the tracks" (Distinctive—Fundamentalist), and the mission (Distinctive—"The Mission") that relates to those who most villagers believed would never be able to get their lives together.

I learned early in my ministry that new arrivals to the village discovered within a short period of time which church they would fit into. Efforts to encourage someone to participate in my church who "knew" he or she would not fit were usually futile. Even those who were attracted by the excellent education program we developed usually did not stay.

It took me longer to recognize why some of the longstanding residents of the village who drew upon my ministry and the ministry of members of my congregation in times of crisis were never able to envision themselves as members of the church of which I was pastor. Try as I might, I was never able to redefine those boundaries. I even discovered that residents who did not participate in any congregation were selectively unchurched.

They knew which church they stayed away from. They knew which church they could fit into if at some point they chose to participate. And if my church was not that church, no matter how deeply they appreciated the ministry other church members and I gave them, they still would not participate.

Social change disrupts even such clearly defined and rigid boundaries. It undermines the connections of churches to the context as well. When the social context in which a congregation is located changes substantially, then its options *and its calling* can no longer be defined simply by recalling its tradition and history. Discovering a possible and faithful future will take more than renewed commitment to old patterns. When a small congregation's traditional place, roles, and relationships are challenged by change, a redoubling of effort alone *rarely* brings about any lasting improvement. *Simply trying harder will not improve the church's situation when the constituencies who found the old style of church life helpful and meaningful have declined, changed, or been replaced.*

When those who surround the small congregation are new or different, leaders need to look beyond their own experience and history to discover the congregation's possible future. They need to consider the changes that confront them and the options that may be open to them within the changes. Each type of social context—rural, fringe, and city neighborhood—has its own characteristic patterns and possibilities. Leaders need to understand the patterns and possibilities inherent in *their* context and to see how congregations faced by the same changes *that they now face* fare when they pursue various options.

When a local social context changes substantially, inevitably the congregations in that context must change as well—and not just because there may be fewer people available to support each of them. Cultures and congregations need much more than memories or shared values or customs to survive. They need roots in their social context. They need the social and economic base that a social context provides. When that social and economic base is eroded, then the culture and the congregation that reflects that culture are also threatened. When the social and economic base is gone, then both congregation and culture continue only among those who can remember the context in which they were once rooted.

Thus, those who live in a trailer in the shadow of an empty and deteriorating farmhouse and those who live as the last survivors of an old, formerly dominant, ethnic group in what has become a pluralistic city neighborhood are both survivors of cultures with uncertain futures. What have the young to look forward to in such circumstances that will enlist their commitment either to church or culture? Only the old who have memories remain committed. Neither a rural culture based on the family farm nor a rural church based on the way of life of those who operate family farms can continue when the family farm is no longer economically viable.

## Summary

In this chapter we have examined the ways congregations connect with their social contexts. We have described small congregations in terms of the social position they occupy in their context—as Dominant, Denominational, and Distinctive. We have looked at the factors associated with congregations' current cultural appeal. We have noted that some congregations include locals more easily, while others relate better to newcomers. A few congregations include a mixture of cultures.

In the chapters that follow we will suggest that small congregations in the midst of change (which include most small congregations today) must find their future within the change at least as much as from their past. The most dependable road that leads to a congregation's future probably begins in its past. But if it ends there, the church is captured by its past. Members of a faithful congregation are not only faithful to their past, but faithful to God who is always present and encouraging them toward a faithful future. They are as clear about their vocation in the present as they are about their roots.

Members of a congregation with a clear sense of vocation develop their potential to minister to the needs that currently surround them. They take the difficulties and possibilities of their social context seriously. They recognize the assets and liabilities of their social position and shape their ministries accordingly. They begin by building on their current appeal, whether it be to locals, newcomers, or a mixture of both. Members of a congregation with a clear vocation accept the fact that they begin with who they are and build on what they have been. And in faith, they move on.

## Questions for Discussion and Reflection

1. Which of the following best describes our congregation's social position?

> Dominant
>
> Denominational
>
> Distinctive

What are the particular difficulties and possibilities associated with our social position?

2. Which of the following best describes our congregation's cultural appeal? Do we appeal more

> to newcomers?
>
> to indigenous persons?
>
> Or are we a culturally mixed group?

What challenges and possibilities are associated with our appeal?

3. In the chart below, place an "x" in the box where your congregation's position and appeal interact.

|  | Newcomer | Indigenous | Culturally Mixed |
|---|---|---|---|
| **Dominant** |  |  |  |
| **Denominational** |  |  |  |
| **Distinctive** |  |  |  |

What possibilities and difficulties emerge when we think of our social position and cultural appeal *together?*

# *Three*
## CHAPTER

# Integrating Community Change into the Small Church

S everal pastors stood in the social gathering during a denominational workshop doing what most professionals do at a meeting that mixes business and pleasure—swapping "war stories" about recent events in their professional lives. They told anecdotes about comic and difficult situations in ministry, shared frustrations about the constant expectations that left them overworked and exhausted, and compared program ideas that seemed promising in the parishes they served.

Eventually the conversation drifted to the subject of membership growth. Some churches were growing, others were not. Now differences became apparent. Pastors of the growing churches spoke with assurance about the effectiveness of their work; pastors of declining churches fell silent, then shifted their conversation briefly to talk about their "spiritual growth." One pastor of a declining urban church needled the pastor of a growing congregation about his absence on a denominational task force on social ethics. The group divided and drifted apart. They were already feeling alienated and were all convinced that their ministries were doing well as long as they were measured by different standards.

With these pastors we were fortunate to have additional information. We had the data to compare the social contexts of their congregations. We could show that growing churches were more likely to be in growing communities and that declining congregations were more likely located in communities where population changes no longer feed the membership of the congregation. In fact, we could show that most growing congregations were not keeping up with the growth potential in their communities—their neighborhoods were growing faster than the church membership. Further, we could show that most declining congregations were retaining members longer than they stayed in the community. Members seemed more loyal and committed to their congregations than in growing communities. When compared with changes in their communities, growing churches were not doing as well, and declining churches were often doing better. Both kinds of churches were a step behind the social changes in the communities they served.

But "comparative success" cannot change the facts of declining membership over time. In the long run, congregations live or die by their relationships to their communities. In the familiar phrasing of H. Paul Douglass, "As the neighborhood goes, so goes the church."[1] Not all churches are dependent upon the immediate neighborhood, but all churches need a source of new members from the community of people they seek to serve.

Demographic differences do have an impact, as we noted in chapter 1. Even the most aggressive congregations have a difficult time attracting young adults to a congregation whose members are an average age of sixty years and older or young families to a church where there is no Sunday church school for children, facilities for infants, or programs for teenagers.

However, demographic data do not reflect the subtle differences in culture between the congregation and the surrounding community(ies). By "culture" we mean the values and behavior that are expected among members of a particular social group. The culture is an unspoken set of assumptions and actions— "the way we do it around here." Attitudes and values may be observed in action, discovered through questions and discus-

[1]H. Paul Douglass, *The Church in the Changing City* (New York: Doran and Company, 1927).

sion, or simply announced in newsletters, from the pulpit, or in other forms of public dialogue. The culture of a group may state one value and live by another—both are genuine parts of the rich mixture of public values and personal choices by which people live. Even more than the objective characteristics of age, gender, income, and education, these cultural differences within and between congregations provide the challenge to release congregational potential.

Evangelism, which is translated as "membership recruitment" by many in ministry, is the single most difficult task for small congregations. If they could recruit members, they would outgrow the "small" description. For many small churches, rapid membership growth is not an option. The prospective members simply are not available or are not responsive to the invitation of the congregation. But most congregations could be numerically stronger in membership and in finances if they used their assets in a more intentional way.

Like most established social institutions, churches are both threatened and nourished by changing populations. They are threatened when the new populations do not share the heritage of the old but, at the same time, must be incorporated into the existing congregational culture. They are threatened when social mobility disrupts the organizational and personal relationships that hold the church together. At the same time, churches are stimulated and nourished by the flow of fresh ideas and energy that new members can bring. The challenge for small church leaders is to mobilize the congregation in response to the threat and enjoy the stimulation, using both to strengthen the life of the congregation.

## The Threat of Changing Communities

The first way in which social mobility threatens congregations is in the challenge of a changing culture. Most congregations were formed to serve the growth or movement of a particular group of people. They were organized initially in the period when the community was first settled, or they came into the community at a time of population growth to serve the religious needs of a particular cultural group. In general, the more the congregation is embedded in a particular historical moment and specific social group, the more difficult it will be for it to adjust and capture the imagination of the next generation or cultural group.

The "birth experience" of most congregations is carried up front in congregational memory, and it does not take much encouragement for members of the church to retell the "myth" to anyone willing to listen. We call the birth experience a "myth" because it is grounded in a few facts which may be interpreted to explain the past in such a way that they give the congregation identity in the present and confidence to face the future.

Generally the founding myth follows a similar pattern: that a few people struggled to begin this congregation or bring it to this place against difficult odds, moving with the Spirit to survive and sometimes prosper. The names of key figures are remembered with honor. Early locations of worship are recalled, and initial traumatic experiences recounted, although the original buildings may have disappeared in the growth of the larger community. The most powerful of these birth stories usually are not told from the pulpit, but are recounted in the informal life of the congregation.

These birth stories are retold when the congregation is faced with difficult decisions, such as whether to develop a new ministry or to change their attitude toward the community. They are also recalled and relived in times of crises and transitions, such as the choice of a pastor or the death of a beloved member and congregational saint. These early stories are the stuff of belonging, and new pastors or prospective members are not really included in "our church family" until they too can "recall" the founding myth of the congregation.

As most local church historians have learned, these stories are not bound by fact. Yet they provide functional memories to unify and motivate the congregation in the present. The memory and retelling of the birth experience can bind a congregation together by feelings of a shared struggle and a common history. At the same time, it can also limit the number of people who are willing to claim a common heritage and are permitted to "re-member" themselves in the retelling of the story. Memory is always binding; it can include new members or exclude them, depending on the skills of leaders and attitudes of members.

Small churches that serve only a small segment of the larger population are particularly vulnerable to the limitations of their own memories. "We have all sorts of people in this church," one old-timer repeated as we looked out at a sea of white heads in a congregational gathering. She seemed to feel that the congregation was inclusive simply because it included members of both sexes (mostly female) who had a wide variety of social perceptions and psychological responses. But they were virtually all over sixty years old, from a single racial, cultural, and language background—in stark contrast with the young and multicultural community (like the St. Luke's church described earlier) that had recently moved into the neighborhood where her church was located. Secure in the strength of their own culture, such churches are often bound by their blindness to other people, and they are limited by the number of people they can imagine caring about their struggle and sharing in their history. This is similar to some of the congregations described in chapter 1. They feel so comfortable with themselves that they resist granting entry to their story to anyone except "birth-right" members, in addition to a small but significant group of others who give the appearance of diversity, but often in fact are more committed to the core values of the group than many lifelong members.

Our recommendation for such congregations begins with the discovery that their congregational story is but a tributary in the great flow of Christian history—special and important, but not completely isolated from the larger church. The small church must respect its own history; many do not because of their feelings of loss and worthlessness. Many feel their story is completely unique or not worth telling to outsiders. Prospective members cannot enter until the church reaffirms its own value and the validity of its own history. At the same time, as the church comes to believe it itself, it must honor the experiences of prospective members and listen to their experiences as a common journey with different events. Together the old members and the newcomers share a sense of God's unfolding purpose in a particular time and place. A feeling of linkage and partnership in a larger purpose is an important element in congregational strength and, perhaps, in numerical growth.

The second way in which social mobility hurts the church is through the social and emotional vacuum that departing members leave in the network of relationships that knit together the life and work of the congregation. The vulnerability of the church is reflected in a pastor's lament, "The 'best people' in our church are most vulnerable to transfer by the corporation or most attracted to new employment in a distant place. The new Sunday school superintendent or chairperson for the financial campaign—the most exciting young leaders of the church—are the same people who catch the eye of management and job placement agencies."

For all churches the loss of leaders is disruptive to the committees and organizations of the church and challenges the institution to find others who can take the places of those who depart. For the small church the loss of personnel is especially difficult. There are fewer people to draw from in the leadership pool of a small-membership church, and everyone is already carrying a variety of responsibilities. Even more, small congregations are more likely to function through the strength of personal relationships than through the authority vested in particular offices. Thus the group leader who leaves may be replaced in the organizational structure of the church; but more important, his or her friends will grieve personally over the loss. One pastor complained, "I can fill the job, but I can't replace the person." In a small congregation the lost leader may have been touching more lives more deeply than is typical in a larger congregation, and the grief takes longer to absorb. Change in leadership is more than an organizational crisis. The personal loss in the smaller church is especially painful and must be faced and admitted before grief can be turned into action.

## The Positive Use of Community Transition

The facts of changing populations cannot be avoided. Some of this change reflects the ebb and flow of economic and social conditions of the community. Even these tough realities can be a source of strength for sensitive congregations. Neighborhood churches are the first to feel the impact of shifting populations. Eventually regional and special-interest congregations will be affected by community changes. The specific background and prior status of a congregation either may be a liability or may become its greatest resource.

When a congregation is frozen in its past successes, change comes as a threat—socially, organizationally, psychologically, economically, and spiritually. In some studies we have seen that the transition of a church from the past to the future is directly related to the loss of previous members—the fewer the members of the previous congregation who remain, the greater the possibility that the emerging congregation will become viable in the new population.[2] However, history does not need to be a handicap. Of all congregations, small churches are especially adept at utilizing their past as a bridge to the future.

As an institution grounded in stability and continuity, the small church is especially threatened both by members leaving and by new members coming in. Clearly, the departure of members leaves the church with fewer people from which to draw leaders and resources. At the same time, the arrival of newcomers is not an assurance that new people are available to take the places of those who have departed. Absorbing new members is an emotional transition that seems especially difficult in smaller churches. Because of their size, they are most vulnerable to the

[2]See materials on churches in transition, such as James H. Davis and Woodie W. White, *Racial Transition in the Church* (Nashville: Abingdon Press, 1980). Also Carl S. Dudley, "Neighborhood Churches in Changing Communities," *New Conversations,* vol. 3 no. 1 (Spring 1978).

loss of leaders. Because of their intimacy, they are more difficult to enter. As the population in a community increases its mobility, small congregations suffer from the loss more acutely.

However, this sense of history, which seems such a liability to some congregations, has been the greatest strength for other churches. In these churches adept leaders have found a way to utilize their *buildings, relationships,* and *stories* in the dynamics of community change.

## Buildings

The church building is often seen as an anchor of community feelings, a symbol of stability in the midst of change. Some congregations have taken this historical function as their only role and have viewed all change with alarm. They are proud to be the monument on the corner, sometimes symbolized by tower clock and chimes. Not all churches have a significant location or historic architecture, but the building with all its memories may provide for many members a spiritual and psychic anchor.

In times of population growth and transition, church buildings have often provided a historical umbrella that transcends the divisions between generations and sets the present tensions and crises in a larger historical context. Some churches provide an inescapable and deeply comforting symbol of continuity and stability through the architecture and heavy construction of the building. "Thank God, it looks like a church," said one non-member who came to the church for counseling, "especially the steeple with its 'thumbs up' to human dignity in praise of the divine."

Church buildings often provoke a curiously ambivalent response, sometimes within the same people. Some people see the church as an antiquated institution with mossbacked memories of bygone days; yet the same people may return to the building with an idealized image of the "real church," which offers a foundation of values for community living and a resource for personal counseling.[3] They tend to push the church to the margins of their consciousness, but keep it handy for counseling, celebrations, and other transitions in their lives. Such people may be "friends of the church" who need it in the community but will not become active members.

As Bruce Reed has pointed out,[4] many people live in the shadow of the steeple as vicarious Christians who will not join the church, but who gain from its very presence affirmation and strength for positive living in the rest of their lives. For them, the church is more important as a symbol than for any specific activity it sponsors. Such people will often financially support the church and its ministries even though they are not officially members. They are sources of strength in the extended church family, needing pastoral care and offering substantial resources, even without official status as members.

## Relationships

In the dynamics of social change, the major contribution of many congregations resides in their ability to provide the symbolic continuity of relationships within a community, to the memories of significant people, and to the places where those memories are stored. I (CSD) remember the church member we visited who invited us to come outside of the church building to "meet my family." We did not know he had family and followed him outside to a lovely church cemetery where his wife and two children were buried. Not all "memory tapes" are so dramatic, but significant places have a therapeutic effect on us all and provide reminders that strengthen our present commitments and encourage us to face the future with confidence.

The small church is often an essential source for the kinds of relationships that are especially helpful in times of conflict and transition. Continuity does not happen automatically.

For further discussion see Carl S. Dudley, *Where Have All Our People Gone? New Choices for Old Churches* (New York: The Pilgrim Press, 1979), p. 39 and following. Also see Wade Clark Roof and William McKinney, *American Mainline Religion* (New Brunswick: Rutgers University Press, 1987).
[4]Bruce Reed, *Dynamics of Religion* (London: Darton, Longman and Todd, 1978).

Churches that shape community identity must be aggressive in stating their views to the community. Some begin with their architecture and location, showing how the congregation and its members have contributed to community history. Other churches build relationships in their spiritual and social ministries as a basis for gathering people and shaping the future. The difference, as one pastor explained it, lies in the larger purpose of church activities: "Our programs are not an end in themselves and are not just a way to build larger church membership and attendance. We are weaving a network of significant personal relationships that will continue to have an impact on this community long after our tasks have been completed and our programs forgotten." Beyond traditional religious resources, some congregations shape community consciousness by retelling appropriate segments of the community history to show that the courage and creativity of the past are needed again in the present.

### Stories

In one way or another all churches mobilize the foundational stories of Christian faith and commitment to meet the challenge of new situations. The physical symbolism of the building and the relationships of people, places, and acts of faithful living come into focus most often in the stories that people remember and retell. Community identity is most clearly recognized in the stories that people tell about themselves and their experiences together. Many churches are very effective storytellers—using sermons, festivals, and publications and remembering community crises and victories long after other segments of the community have forgotten. Congregations have a significant opportunity to become the arena for sharing stories—stories of the old-timers who remember how the community was shaped in the past, as well as stories of the newcomers who have experiences to share from other situations.

Stories provide such a significant way to transcend differences and create new community commitments that we use the technique of sharing personal stories in the next section as one basic resource in aiding the cultural mix of old-timers and newcomers.

## Old-Timers and Newcomers

Every congregation confronts the challenge of integrating the old-timers with the newcomers and vice versa. Not all are as troubled as some of the congregations we discussed in chapter 1, but the challenge exists in every congregation. It is sometimes escalated when the children of members feel alienated by the culture of the congregation and attracted by cultural values outside the church. Children may reflect more the values of their companions than the commitments of their parents. They are part of the larger challenge—that congregations must bridge the cultural gap between church and community in order to receive new members.

The "natives" are comfortable with one another. They may not all be pleasant to one another, but they know everyone in the community if not personally, then through their connections. These long-term residents know the networks that hold people together. As old-timers, they know the history of a community and the distinctive culture of the congregation. They have a language among themselves that outsiders cannot quite duplicate. They speak with broad "a's" and rolled "r's" and omitted "t's" in such a way that they can recognize a kind of intimacy even in a pattern of speech.

Although there may be vast differences among the natives, they resemble each other more than they resemble the new outsiders. They may not be able to explain their differences, yet they share a kind of common experience that holds them together. They often remember the deepest experiences not in explanation, but in silence. In the term "the sacrament of silence" Ivan Illich[5] reminds us of the importance of the unspoken awareness among people who have shared experiences

[5]Ivan D. Illich, *Celebration of Awareness: A Call for Institutional Revolution* (New York: Doubleday and Co., 1970), especially chapter 4, "The Eloquence of Silence."

across the years. They may have fewer of the world's material goods to live on, but in the communion of shared experience they make what they have go further.

By contrast, as we noted in chapter 2, newcomers are "from away." Although they may be self-assured in their own world, they seem awkward and out of place in the world of the old-timer. Lacking the past of shared experience, they seek to form alliances through creating new projects. Frequently the newcomers bring cosmopolitan values from a larger world that clash distinctively with the values and behavior of the local congregation. Typically, newcomers are more apt to attend meetings on time rather than by the more casual schedule of the natives. They are more likely to dress up for a social occasion than to dress down to the informality of the natives. Because newcomers often have moved into the area in response to economic opportunity, they are apt to have more formal education than the locals, to hold more professional jobs, and to be younger in the family cycle. For all these reasons there is a natural distance between newcomers and old-timers. Both geographically and psychologically, newcomers are considered "from away" by the natives.

In many situations longtime members reflect the history or past of the area and the newcomers represent its future. In an exchange of gifts, each may recognize their need for what the other has to give. Many newcomers would like to share the heritage and traditions of the communities into which they move. They want to be accepted into the story, at least temporarily, while they are there. Of course they don't want it exactly the way it was, but they do want some elements preserved. In fact, newcomers often are more enthusiastic about maintaining the heritage of the past than many people who have been there long enough to recognize its limitations. Depending on which group is more vocal, some congregations become dominated by the energy and arrogance of newcomers, and some retain the character and limitations of the old-timers.

Effective evangelism must bridge the gap between newcomers and locals. There are many approaches to this challenge. Here we mention four basic resources that leaders can use to bring the tension of cultural differences into constructive dialogue. The first two are general resources that can be applied in many areas, and the other two are more specific activities for bridging the old and the new.

## Organizational Activities

Churches frequently want the energy and the economic support of new members, but do not know how to assimilate them into the congregational culture. One approach to assimilating newcomers is through the common ground of organizational activities. Smaller congregations try to assimilate the newcomers into the existing groups and activities. After all, there are not many groups, and every warm body is appreciated for the sharing of the work load. However, newcomers who do not honor the past often find themselves unwelcome.

Larger congregations can assimilate many newcomers by creating new tasks with new purposes. Thus, goal setting is one means of evangelism, creating many activities that need active support to accomplish. Frequently the wide variety of groups in a larger church reflects clusters of members who have joined at a particular time and move like waves on the ocean through the life of the congregation. The values and behavior (subculture) of the church often reflect the values that were dominant at particular moments as newcomers have come in with each new generation. Larger congregations often contain the "waves" of adult Sunday school classes or specialized activities that began with a particular generation of newcomers and have continued to sustain that population through the life of the congregation. The congregation may provide a larger umbrella of identity, but the deepest commitment of members may be to the smaller group to which they've belonged over the years.

Many smaller congregations do not have the luxury of creating new groups for each class of new members. In their small church with great needs, new members must be assimilated into the existing patterns of congregational life. Such assimilation may be possible occasionally, but generally requires something more than the expansion of new groups or other simple organizational adjustments. Smaller congregations need to bring new members into the congregational culture. Larger congregations accomplish organizational expansion through additional groups.

## Shared Memories

A second method of assimilation is through the shared memories of common stories. In his study of synagogue life, Samuel Heilman has identified the importance of shared stories.[6] In the intimacy of a small congregation it is important that stories be shared to affirm the values that hold the congregation together. Stories are often retold about the lives of members, some of whom have long since departed. The purpose of the stories is to affirm the sense of belonging and to rehearse the values that hold the congregation together.

Newcomers can bring their own stories to enrich the life of the church, but they must also absorb the memories that hold the congregation together. Unfortunately, many prospective members do not slow down long enough to hear the local church stories. They are so oriented to programs and the productive use of time that they do not recognize the importance of listening to the significant stories of the longtime church members. Sensitive pastors can help, but new members must want to listen and to share their histories.

## Annual Events

A third approach makes use of annual events that provide a kind of birthday party for the old-timers in the church. These celebrations provide time for the congregation to remember its stories and sing its songs. Annual events often embrace a much larger membership than those who are on the rolls of the church. For many small congregations, annual events are the

---

[6]Samuel Heilman, *Synagogue Life: A Study in Symbolic Interaction* (Chicago: University of Chicago Press, 1973).

way in which the congregation affirms that it belongs to a place and among a people by retelling the stories and sharing the experiences that have shaped them through the years.

New and prospective members find that annual events provide the arena and atmosphere in which they can feel "inducted" into the stories and invited to share the rhythm and pace of the congregational culture. Small churches do not have to have different activities for every age and gender group in the congregation. They have fewer activities, but they should be of greater significance and be remembered and shared among the congregation. One purpose of the church, said Henri Nouwen, is "to create events worth remembering."[7] Annual events are an excellent time to bring new people into the memory of congregational stories.

Anniversaries and birthdays provide an occasion for sharing the past, mixing cultural backgrounds, and transcending generational differences. In the stories swapped in such events, the outsider is welcomed into the past, especially if he or she has a story to share. Samuel Heilman maintains that stories are the currency of exchange in the heart of congregational life.[8] As one delightfully candid member admitted, "It's not hardly worth going to church without hearing a few good stories."

## Remembered History

Fourth, in a more formal way, a "night of remembrance" may also be used to bring newcomers into the flow and stories of congregational memory. As described in *The Handbook for Congregational Studies,*[9] the night of remembrance is a celebration in the life of a congregation for remembering those events and persons who have shaped the congregation and in whom their memories are anchored. Such a night of remembrance can reach back to the formative experiences of congregational life

[7]Henri J. Nouwen, *Creative Ministry* (New York: Doubleday and Co., 1971), see especially chapter 5, "Celebrating."
[8]Samuel Heilman, *Synagogue Life: A Study in Symbolic Interaction,* chap. 5, "Gossip."
[9]*Handbook for Congregational Studies* (Nashville: Abingdon Press, 1986), pp. 24–25.

and reach forward in the hopes and expectations of contemporary members. It can show the critical moments of crisis that the congregation has faced and the patterns of conflict and solution that have been typical in this congregation's history. In the night of remembrance the congregation can recall those saints in their history who gave themselves in a previous era to make the congregation more fully Christian. In these examples and models, members can recall the ways in which they have been shaped by particular experiences, and they can plan the future using well-worn patterns of congregational behavior. Conflict, planning, and problem solving are far more consistent in the history of a congregational culture than even the particular personalities who engage in these activities. Newcomers bring their own stories to the life of the church, but they must join the past before they can participate fully in the present.

In a wonderfully detailed study, Jim Hopewell suggests that every congregation enacts a lived story reflecting the values and commitments of its members.[10] With the setting, plot, and characters established by the patterns and values of congregational life, the members feel drawn to reenact the story in each new crisis and challenge. Hopewell says that the patterns of the congregational story (as in literature) contain a combination of comic, tragic, romantic, and ironic elements in the development of the plot. Once the pattern of the story is established, it will be repeated until the removal (moving, retirement, or death) of a major figure allows for new development in the story of that congregation. Such fixed patterns of thought and behavior challenge the common view that congregations are only "voluntary" associations, but are recognized by numerous consultants, pastors, and members who have visited many congregations — each with an established personality and character all its own. As in friendship, you must know the character of the church before you can feel at home in its presence.

[10]James F. Hopewell, *Congregation: Stories and Structures* (Philadelphia: Fortress Press, 1987).

## Past and Future as Orientations to Faith

Although the concept of newcomers and old-timers provides a helpful framework for understanding the dynamics within and between congregations, sometimes these terms encourage stereotypes that do not fit the personalities of individual long-time members and newcomers to the community and congregation. The pastors to whom we referred in the opening session of this chapter discovered significant differences among individuals with whom they worked in the church and community. One useful distinction was found in their orientation toward time. They found that the sense of belonging to a community is experienced differently by people who see it through the eyes of the past—what it has been—and by people who see it through the expectations of the future—what it might become.

The distinction between people who look to the past and those who look to the future has some similarities with the tensions between old-timers and newcomers. Yet the distinction is important because it liberates the longtime members and newcomers from predetermined orientations. Some old-timers who might be expected to be locked into the past are very future oriented. Conversely, some newcomers, who have only the future to share, have a nostalgia for a past they have never experienced. When we use "past" and "future" as tools of analysis, we can better understand differences and tensions within the church without trying to describe or stereotype the lifestyle of particular people who happen to be old-timers and newcomers. These two perspectives approach faith differently.

### Grounded in the Past

For people oriented toward past experience, faith is a network of relationships that preexist our awareness, symbolized by the baptism of infants. Their faith is a community consciousness that provides the context in which the individual finds identity. Faith, therefore, is carried by the group, by the significant relationships that are remembered in the community of

faith. Because of its ties to community, we call this faith perspective *relational.* Because they tune into the feelings that
unite the community, we call those who share this faith "affec-
tional Christians."

## Shaping the Future

By contrast, people who find faith in the challenge of shaping
the future place a greater emphasis on their individual religious
commitment to live according to God's purposes. In this perspective the community does not preexist the individual, but is
composed of various people who agree (contract) to work together for individual contributions toward a common goal.
Because of their commitment to a purpose, we call this perspective *directional.* Because of the discipline required for commitment to that goal, we call those who share this perspective
"rigorous Christians."

Relational faith is a past-history experience in which the
individual is carried by the group. Directional faith is based on
the commitment of individuals who compose the group to
shape "future history" as they feel called by God. As Max
Weber noted, it is the difference between those individuals who
see themselves as a "vessel" (carrier) of faith and those who see
themselves as a "tool" (instrument) in the hand of God.[11]

The concept of a relational faith helps us to understand the
strength and durability of many small congregations.[12] It helps
explain the core commitments of many longtime members who
share a faith that is carried by their attachments to particular
people and special "sacred" places. People with this orientation
find satisfaction in gatherings of believers who reinforce each
other by being together. Their relational faith enjoys the release

---

[11]See a wide range of parallel comparisons in G. H. Mueller, "Asceticism and
Mysticism," *International Yearbook for the Sociology of Religion* (1973), pp. 68–132.
Also see "The Protestant and the Catholic Ethic," *Annual Review of the Social Sciences
of Religion* (1978), 2:143-66.

[12]This concept provided the basis for Carl S. Dudley, *Making the Small Church
Effective* (Nashville: Abingdon Press, 1978).

of emotions in a common celebration as the acme of religious expression. People who have grounded their faith in relationships with other people understand that the faith is carried through family and home, through local customs and language, through memories of the past and hopes for future generations. The relational faith of small congregations is carried by their traditions and rhythms of life, by an unbroken flow of events that evokes a sacramental sense of divine permanence.

By contrast, those of a rigorous, more directional faith reflect the individualism and ambition of the larger society outside the intimacy of many small churches. Such people are trained to believe in progress, that they can create a "better world." Not emotional release, but restraint is their goal. Their highest emotion is not celebration, but esthetic denial, the work ethic that can make a difference in the world. Directional Christians with an expectation of significant changes see faith in the commitment of individuals toward immediate, significant improvements in their lives. Their faith is affirmed by change and satisfied by a creative sense of achievement. Thus relational faith can survive in a stable or declining economy, while rigorous faith implies and often asserts a constant growth of economic possibilities.

Our pastors found that newcomers tend to be more rigorous and longtime members tend to be more relational. But some manifestation of each perspective exists in every congregation. The people of rigorous faith tend to be the organizers and managers of our churches. The people of relational faith provide the social glue that holds the congregation together. Creative congregational programs maintain mutual respect and a working alliance between these two understandings of faith.

## Misunderstandings

However, these two perspectives can seriously misunderstand each other. The pastors noted that in the business meetings the rigorous people wanted to get in and get out and the more relational members wanted to spend the time catching up on the neighbors. They felt the tensions in planning worship when some rigorous members wanted creativity and some relational people enjoyed the casual continuity with the past. They saw it in the selection of church school teachers: some members emphasized the need for "real teachers" and others wanted "real people" (and pastors were generally grateful to take whoever was available). The pastors reflected the difference in their own approach to pastoral care. Some were more professionally rigorous, giving pastoral care in the office. Others were more informally relational and contacted persons wherever available, wishing to see people in the context of their whole life—at home, work, and leisure. In the workshop with these pastors we talked of the tensions between these two perspectives in every aspect of ministry from in-house administration to community-based social ministries.

Disciplined, rigorous faith often pronounces judgment on the social orientation of the relational approach. Rigorous faith often sees the relational faith as aimless and irresponsible and wishes the relational person were more organized and less haphazard. The rigorous perspective often urges the church to be more purposeful and less of a "social club." For the rigorous believers, the more relational person often seems accommodating and passive in the face of social change. The rigorous person may honor but not enter the intimacy of group experience. To "help" the relational believer, the rigorous believer offers insight for "enlightenment."

Relational faith often responds to such "help" by feeling that the rigorous approach seems lonely, intellectual, and unfeeling, hard to know and difficult to share. Rigorous pastors tend to be stoic about their illnesses and continue to work anyway. Since such rigorous behavior denies feelings of illness or weakness, relational people feel alienated, sometimes unloved. Relational believers honor the energy and commitment of the rigorous, but wonder if they will ever accomplish their varied goals. Even as the rigorous person enjoys numbers and productivity, the relational person finds the reporting of numerical success to be intimidating to the group and irrelevant to the significant

Christian relationships. For example, the most "productive" pastors were seen as ambitious, tense, and unnatural to the more feeling-based relational Christians. Perhaps most challenging of all, the relational church members were concerned that rigorous believers did not share their deepest faith, which had to be *experienced in community.*

At worst, this tension can tear apart the local church seeking to respond to its social context. The battles within the congregation can be escalated by the sense of righteousness that each perspective can engender.

## *Program*

At best, this tension between the past and the future allows us to more widely encompass all orientations found in the Christian faith. Programs built on rigorous *and* relational dimensions can draw together both the organizational and the human dimensions of cultural continuity. In our work with the group of pastors, we had to generate evangelism programs that developed both the clarity of faith for the rigorous believer and the arena of sharing for the more relational orientation. Our preaching needed to contain the faith articulated and grounded in careful scholarship, but also needed to be supported by the stories of particular people known to members in the congregation. In programs of Christian education, congregations became concerned both with the content of the teaching and with the relationships that developed among members in the class.

At the same time, also, we have found that this distinction between rigorous and relational helps church leaders to understand why some congregations treat their history and location quite differently from others. New churches, suburban congregations, and churches in racially changing communities tend to be more rigorous than relational, especially when they have a high turnover of membership. The organizational structures of these churches provide a more stable framework for a variety of people to find their places within the life of the congregation.

Most small churches are dominated by a relational lifestyle, but must survive in a world dominated by more rigorous approaches. Old churches in city and rural areas and ethnic/racial congregations generally tend to be more relational than rigorous. The culture they are carrying tends to be embodied in a particular network of relationships that carry the faith beyond any explanations. The culture within the church is often at odds with the culture without. Each of these perspectives (rigorous and relational) sees history appropriately—one begins with the future and the other begins with the past.

## Tensions in Context

The differences between rigorous and relational expressions of Christian faith become evident in the leadership and programming of each pair of congregations that we introduced in the first chapter.

In the rural area, the First Church in Matthewstown is more bound by relationships among people and to a place, more grounded in the past than pressing toward the future. Its members think of change in terms of generational care, not organizational goals, more in terms of goals for the decades than accomplishments each month or each year. By contrast, the Marksburg Church in the fringe area has a stronger mix of those who measure their lives by building toward the future and those who find primary satisfactions in sustaining relationships of the past. Such members are aware of the tension and often flirt with the option, though the longstanding members of the Marksburg church finally chose to cling to old relationships and restore the symbols of the past. Pastors in such settings need to be more aware of the tensions between the future and the past, between rigorous and relational styles of expressing the Christian faith.

In city churches we note similar and even sharper contrasts between the extended family, informal lifestyle of an ethnic-minority church and the challenging, upwardly mobile style of the St. Luke's church in a redevelopment area. An ethnic-

minority church has the accumulated momentum of generations of cultural identity carried in patterns of behavior, rituals
of worship, smells of cooking, and intonations of language. In
the best of all possible worlds, they gain new members by birth
or, second best, by marriage. As the ethnic base of the church
community disperses, the congregations suffer. By contrast,
redevelopment congregations like St. Luke's must move more
toward management through task groups, so that new members
can join with them in creating a future, not just sustaining a
past. Theirs is the culture of change, and the absence of change
often makes them uncomfortable, restless, and sometimes ready
to move on. These two city churches, even on the same corner,
would demand very different leadership and programs.

The fringe churches like Marksburg provide a cultural mix,
but for an often unanticipated reason: some of the most mobile
people now want to put down roots and remain. The typical
suburban congregation is bedrock (home) for some families and
a stepping-stone for others. Some members want to put down
roots and establish lasting relationships; they want to create a
relational community by living close together. Other members
are still psychologically on the road, still mobile in their minds
if not in their economic possibilities. They want more to share
the rigorous tasks of ministry than to live closely together. Such
suburban congregations are constantly weaving together the
themes of past and future.

The exurban congregation of the more distant fringe is more
clearly defined, but no less a mixture. The longtime members
are often entrenched, but willing to let newcomers become
officers and church leaders "as long as they don't change any-
thing important." Newcomers, who have taken the bold step to
move far from the urban center, would like to take on the values
of the "rural life," but are ingrained in a lifetime of disciplined
planning for the future. These members often seem like ships
that pass in the night—they would like to accommodate each
other, but have little language by which to communicate and
appreciate the values that make them experience life differently.

Releasing the potential of both perspectives demands the most sensitive skills of leadership in both pastors and lay leaders.

## Leadership

The task of the pastor and other congregational leaders is to honor the past while being responsive creatively to trends of the future. This often means that leadership must provide what is least available. For congregations that are more relational, leaders may need to be more disciplined and rigorous. For congregations that are more rigorous, leaders may need to provide the relational glue. The dialogue between newcomers and longtime members is a significant part of a much larger dynamic in the life of a church. This larger dynamic involves the geographic and historical location of the church and decisions about the culture that it seeks to maintain.

## Summary

In this chapter we have tried to show that congregations are not simply a static product of their particular location. Rather, they reflect the influence of the community and provide a base for continuity within the necessity for change.

In the process of change, newcomers entering a congregation can bring a vitality and strength. They can be a threat to old members and be prohibited from making their contribution to the church. Or they can be incorporated into the culture-carrying congregation by allowing the congregation to take pride in its past. When church leaders are willing to open the past, new members may participate more fully.

In program development, the tension between rigorous and relational provides the energy to transcend and unify cultural diversity. Rigorous commitments bring vision and energy for change. Relational faith provides a network and stability within which change is possible. The combination of rigorous and relational provides the dynamic that balances both stability and change in program and leadership development. Sensitivity to this tension can help to prevent the imposition of inappropriate models and can affirm the combination of cultural styles that seem right for each congregation as it ministers in its community context.

## Questions for Discussion and Reflection

### Congregational History

1. Do you know the congregation's beginnings—its founding myth? In how many versions? When has this story been told, who tells it, and for what purpose?

2. What are some critical moments and significant events in the history of the church? What are the mountaintop experiences in congregational memory? What are the dark valleys of challenge and conflict?

3. Who are the central figures, the important people, and the memorable personalities in congregational history?

4. What values and behavior (culture) are embodied in the memories of these events and individuals? What are the implications for contemporary behavior and decisions?

### Entry Points

1. What organizations and group activities are being created to absorb new members and reinforce existing friendship patterns?

2. What possibilities are given to new and prospective members to hear the stories of the church and to share stories of their own?

3. What annual events bring the church (and community) together? How can these be used to celebrate congregational history, retell its story in a positive light, and open it up for others to join?

### Past and Future Orientations to Faith

1. Which church leaders (including the pastor) are more oriented to relationships in the past, and which leaders are oriented to achievements in the future? What implications does this have for congregational programs and styles of leadership?

2. Is the basic style of congregational life as a whole more relational and grounded in the past or more rigorous and measured by goals in the future? Is this orientation shared by new and prospective members? What implications does this have for evangelism and program development?

# *Four*
## CHAPTER

# Small Congregations That Change Communities

S mall congregations are uniquely situated to effect change in their communities. We have already noted the significant impact that the culture has upon churches that are located in rural, fringe, and urban areas. In each of these locales, small churches have different relationships and resources for effecting social change.

In chapter 1 we identified two kinds of churches, each with a unique bond between church and community. These rural and fringe (formerly rural, now becoming suburban) congregations have been battered by seas of social change in the past few years, and both have shown remarkable tenacity in struggling to survive these pressures. Radical changes in agriculture and massive population movements have stripped many rural areas of their vitality and identity as continuing communities.

In rural areas these congregations are often the most viable remaining voluntary organizations. They have seen the rise and fall of many other community groups during their long history. In many areas the grange and the community school are only memories recalled by the tombstones of unpainted buildings that sit empty by the old highway or by engravings on cornerstones in small-town buildings now used for other purposes. But the churches more frequently remain, retaining the legacy of social and economic cooperation from the hard times of a former era. With deep roots in the past and a determination to survive, they have the distinct advantage of being the curators of community memory. "If we don't know," one pastor said about the network of political and social connections in the history of his community, "we know who does—and we can find out."

In urban areas small churches are often blessed with being marginal to the mainstream of the society and thus are free to act with innovative responses to difficult situations. The old ethnic churches retain the traces of extended family bonds, which have kept them together long after the "ma-and-pa" stores of the neighborhood have given way to fast-food franchises and chain stores merchandising everything from groceries to entertainment. Redevelopment congregations are often more culturally mixed, sustained more by a common vision of the future than a common heritage from the past. Both have rich treasuries of historical contacts and memories of the communities in which they are located. Even congregations in transitional areas, where the older members have moved out and the energy comes from newcomers, have memorabilia from previous years of community growth and stories that chronicle the developments of the neighborhood in prior generations.

In city churches the common ground of history often rekindles in a congregation the memories of earlier struggles that are not greatly different from the issues faced by their communities in this generation. In the life of a congregation, memory is not exactly what *happened,* but what is *remembered* in order to explain, shape, and motivate the community in the present. History, through the filters of memory retold in many stories, can provide a variety of bridges to unify people across racial, cultural, and even religious differences. In the intimacy of small churches, such memories are often carefully maintained, as if waiting for the moment when they can be used to shape the future.

The small church can be an agent of change when it offers a common foundation for the diverse segments of a community who are seeking to make their community a more livable place.

One small church in agricultural New England has recalled the struggles of early farmers in the area, drawing on these stories to inspire a memory of "native toughness" that has helped them develop a modern, competitive, small industry in that rural area. One small congregation in a large metropolitan area has used its Scandinavian heritage as a basis for ministry to recently arrived immigrants from Mexico. Although the differences are great, the old immigrant memories are sufficient to bridge to new, yet common, experiences.

Urban and rural church memories have much in common—they are often haunted by the glories of the past. Always, it seems, historic events are enhanced by memory—the "mountaintops" are more glorious and the tough times more terrible. With their energies strained by survival needs, small churches sometimes lose the vision of what's possible when they cling too closely to the past. Biblically, like individual Christians, churches that lose their lives for the sake of the gospel will gain even more (Matthew 16:25; Mark 8:35; Luke 9:24, 17:33). Numerous small churches have found new life when they forgot their own institutional crisis of declining membership and increasing expenses and offered a more positive ministry to unite the community.

One church in a major midwestern city felt it was too small and weak to retain a pastor and maintain Sunday services; so it opened its doors to the elderly on Tuesdays and now maintains (and is maintained by) a booming ministry with senior citizens throughout the area. Another congregation that was located in a deteriorating section of town invested its resources in housing renewal in the area and sparked a renaissance of housing in the area. Both built upon their memories, not of specific programs, but of stories about the energy, risk, and imagination that were embedded in the caring ministries of previous generations.

Suburban and exurban congregations offer another kind of challenge in the involvement of church in social change. Their members are more likely to have separate spaces in their lives for work and for home, for leisure and for religion. These congregations tend to emphasize pastoral care, individual responsibilities, and programs for each different age and interest group in the congregation.

We have already noted the conflict in the fringe setting of an exurban congregation between the newcomers and the longtime members, the "pioneers and homesteaders" as Lyle Schaller has called them.[1] Such conflicts often reflect the social trauma being experienced throughout the community. The strength of the small church is in the scale of its conflict. In these transitional areas, the feelings of the larger community can be heard and identified with particular people; the larger issues can be scaled down and confronted by individuals who know and care for one another. As one pastor said when she was asked to moderate a public meeting in a changing neighborhood: "I believe I can do it all right because I have already heard all the arguments in miniature. We've had the community tempest in our teapot for months."

Suburban and exurban churches often have the contacts to make change possible even when the congregation does not feel called to act as a corporate body. The members of such churches are often professionally prepared and politically situated to help resolve social issues as their consciousness is raised. Further, they often have access to the media when they wish their views to be known. Both pastors and members who hold responsible positions seem to have a special rapport with mobile populations looking for community leadership. The Warrens,[2] in describing their studies in suburban areas, identify the importance of visibility for both congregations and pastors in shaping the values and commitments of highly mobile communities. Church leaders often have a unique access to public consciousness in their efforts to help the larger community see the issues that they face, imagine the possible resolutions of those issues, and trust their capacity to act effectively. When political leaders

[1]See Lyle E. Schaller, *Hey, That's Our Church* (Nashville: Abingdon Press, 1975), p. 93.

[2]Rachelle B. Warren and Donald I. Warren, *The Neighborhood Organizer's Handbook* (Notre Dame, Ind.: University of Notre Dame Press, 1977).

speak, many communities suspect self-interest. When informed pastors and church committees articulate a vision of a possible solution to a community issue, many people would like to believe their objectivity and explore the options they recommend.

Small Denominational churches (see chapter 2), regardless of location, often find that they have access to resources far beyond their immediate fellowship. Members of small churches frequently have personal ties that can be used to link the struggles of the community with people who are in strategic places of power and influence—people who are in the congregation, or more frequently, people who know (or are related to) people who can make things happen. All churches are part of the many networks and relationships of kinfolk and friendships that hold the community together and link it to the larger world. Sometimes the professional help of lawyers, accountants, and teachers from other congregations has been tapped by small churches within the extended family of denominational connections. Some small congregations have brought media attention to needy local situations and found unique pockets of funding for many worthy causes. Small church leaders often provide the unique element of social and religious confidence that helps the community believe that it can act, and that its actions can make a difference.

The impact of Distinctive small churches depends on the orientation of the church toward its culture. Many small congregations take their size as one more reason to resist or escape their culture. Other Distinctive small churches that relate positively to the culture must clarify the unique source of their own unity. Some of the most effective churches dedicated to social transformation are small congregations that are theologically delighted to be different from the world as they find it. Civil rights activist churches in the 1960s, churches against apartheid in the 1970s, and sanctuary churches for Central American political refugees in the 1980s all were drawn disproportionately from the ranks of small congregations that strongly believed in political applications of their Christian convictions.

Distinctive small churches, by their nature, survive by defining themselves as different from other churches and from the world as they see it. Their disagreement with the world is not always expressed in issues of community social concern. Their distinctiveness provides essential energy to mobilize the resources of church members. When that alternative view is focused on social issues, these churches have an impact on the religious, social, and political consciousness of the community and often of the nation far out of proportion to their small membership.

To the pastors and members of these socially committed congregations, their style often seems the only way to witness in particular settings. Such dedication is commendable for its effectiveness, but it is often limited to the duration of particular pastoral leadership. Following their experience in such socially conscious congregations, members often find other congregations less than satisfying. Many ex-members of such churches, when they move to new communities or when the pastoral leadership changes, become alumni of churches as a whole. As one faithful member said, "I'm nostalgic for the excitement of the time when our little 'church militant' was challenging the city fathers. It's never been the same since then, and I doubt if I will ever feel completely satisfied with church membership again."

The categories we have used for churches—rural, fringe, and city churches and the Dominant, Denominational, and Distinctive churches—all develop different but definable patterns by which they influence their communities. Many small churches have a significant impact on the physical health, economic stability, and spiritual vitality of their communities. In some areas they are effective because of their wide connections, in some because they are not captive to the mainstream, and in some because they have retained the capacity for organizational decisions and effective actions. Despite these differences, churches that have a social impact combine certain recognizable characteristics.

## Essential Elements for Effective Action

In many respects churches that have an impact on their communities are no different from other congregations. As we noted in earlier chapters, all small churches are strongly influenced by the communities in which they develop their ministries. The social location of the church is the sea in which the ministry must be lived. It may not determine the character of the congregation, but it sets the framework within which their program and process must make sense. Therefore, churches in the suburbs are different from city or rural congregations, and churches in the South are distinctive from the West Coast or Northeast. Effective and faithful congregations are sensitive to these differences and translate the universal gospel into the local language of the community they seek to reach.

External changes in community life often catch churches off guard. Change may seem inevitable because it results from economic forces, such as shifting patterns of community employment or changes from residential to commercial use of property. The character of a community can be altered when populations grow older without the family cycle including people of all ages, when they experience a change in their spending capacity, or when a shift occurs in the relative proportions of various racial and ethnic groups. Churches must accommodate such changes in the community.

The church can also be an initiator or catalytic agent in the process of community change. The strengths for effecting change are not limited to the inevitable forces of economic and social crisis or the clout of political power. The basic resources for change within the church—and between the church and community—lie in the interrelationship of three elements in the life of the congregation.

### Historical Memory

The more clearly a congregation understands and affirms its role in the past, the more easily it can accept the possibility of change to meet the future. One essential element of congregational social action is the ability to recall the strength of Christian faith and the specific journey through which the congregation has come and from that to lift up appropriate models that generate energy and commitment to a constructive future.

## Social Vision

A community cannot accomplish what it cannot imagine. One essential contribution that a congregation can make is to help the community envision what it would like to become. Such a social vision should have roots in the broad faith and particular memories of the congregation. It should have the excitement of an experience yet unrealized and the possibilities of commitment worth the sacrifice.

## Decisive Action

In addition to the identity from the past and the vision of the future, the congregation must believe it has the capacity to achieve the goal to which it aspires. It must be able to make decisions and to act upon its decisions. One essential element of social action is the organizational capacity for the congregation to make and keep its commitments.

Thus, leadership in congregations that effect change in their communities includes interdependence among those people who remember the past, those who envision the future, and those who have the capacity to act in the present.

## Overemphasis on One Element

Some congregations emphasize one of these elements to the detriment of others. For example, some churches major in their own history. Churches of all sizes, not just small churches, may be inclined toward this problem, but small churches sometimes become captive to their own cuteness, like a picture on a Christmas card or a nostalgic memory that dominates the present. For example, the First Church building in Matthewstown (chapter 1) was reconstructed to evoke another era; in another church perhaps the liturgy and ritual are maintained to allow the worshiper to step back in time. In some churches even the pictures on the walls and the stories that members tell reflect an earlier generation, sometimes as much as a century or more past. Such congregations are rooted so deeply in the past that nothing of the present shows above ground. Denham Grierson suggests that such churches are "living under time."[3]

I once worked with a congregation that had an annual bazaar of secondhand items for which they erected a large sign reading "White Elephant Sale." One irreverent neighbor, who often condemned the congregation for living in the past, asked if the church were up for sale, "the real white elephant of the community," he announced. Many churches are like that sign—living in a past time of seemingly greater glory.

Some congregational leaders urge a vision of the future of the church without first finding a way to interpret their hopes within the history and experience of the church. As we noted in the story of the Marksburg church in chapter 1, this oppression of an ideal is especially a problem with outsiders, newcomers, and clergy who are on the move. They do not know the traditions and stories of the congregation, but enter with an agenda for action already prepared to be plugged into the ongoing life of the church. They almost assure failure for their proposals, and, what's worse, they blame it all on the congregation for not seeing it their way.

There is no magic period of time required for entry into the life of the congregation, any more than a predefined period of courtship can assure a happy marriage. But for new pastors to attempt to make even the most basic changes during the initial months of a ministry (during the "honeymoon" as it is often called) frequently wounds the relationship and leaves scars that never completely disappear. Longtime members of an Episcopal church near a seminary call this behavior the "curate's

[3]Denham Grierson, *Transforming a People of God* (Melbourne: The Joint Board of Christian Education of Australia and New Zealand, 1984).

complex" because they see it happen so frequently with fired-up seminarians in their first parish assignment.

Some members develop a fascination with the organizational structure of the congregation. Avery Dulles has identified the "institution" as one way people relate to their church.[4] Carried to an extreme, some members "love the church." They love some expression of the church in its building or its sanctuary or the room where their class meets (has met for years) or its organizational board or the responsibility to count the money or some other specific place, activity, or group of people. For these members, the physical and social structure of the church may be more important than the history and heritage that is already past or the uncharted future that has yet to be experienced.

People who are committed to the structure and organization of the church are among the most faithful and supportive members—always present when the doors are open and generous when the congregation needs a helping hand or financial support. Yet in working with congregations we often find the possibilities of change frustrated by people who "love the church." They may oppose a youth program because young people will mess up the building and may oppose sharing the building with a day-care program or another congregation because the other groups "do not appreciate what we have sacrificed to develop the good things we have around here."

Memory, vision, and structure can be idols when worshiped alone, but when balanced together they are the basic elements in the chemistry of change.

### Historical Memory as a Resource for Change

Congregations can face the present and shape the future based on the most positive use of historical memory. Memory

---

[4]Avery Dulles, *Models of the Church* (Garden City, N.Y.: Doubleday and Co., 1974), chapter 2. Dulles's models have proven insightful for many congregations, large and small.

is carried in the stories people tell about personalities who have shaped the life of the church, the challenges and crises that they met, and the funny, mundane behavior associated with these people. Some characters in the story of the church's past are heroes and heroines—bigger than life in their decisions and their commitments. Some characters are simple, faithful people who lived out the story of the church and helped to move it through transitional times.

Such memories can carry a congregation for a long time. Recently we gathered leaders from a number of churches to consider the influence of their history on the life of the congregation today.[5] One local congregational historian in central Illinois commented that the people who organized her congregation "were strong, God-fearing individuals who took dedicated stands against national and local injustice . . . for women's suffrage (1841), against timber stealing (1842) and strongly opposed to slavery (1848)." Another church leader from Indiana stretched the congregation's memory even further, noting, "The church has made several changes since 1827, . . . but one thing is for sure: if it involves people who need help, this church will be there." Sometimes particular people are remembered in the history of the church, such as local heroes and heroines of a crisis well past or national and denominational figures who shaped the thinking of the church. Sometimes the central, dominating figure is Jesus of Nazareth, in whose shadow the church was formed.

Memory is not necessarily recalling exactly what happened, but what the congregation selects to remember. History may be the facts, but memory is often shaped to fit the challenge that faces the congregation at the moment. Thus church leaders can choose which events to celebrate in shaping the character of the congregation and whose stories to repeat in times of celebration. The church that remembers Dorothy Day and Walter

[5]Quotes that follow are taken from materials of the Church and Community Project sponsored by the Center for Congregational Ministries of McCormick Theological Seminary in the spring of 1987.

Rauschenbusch is far more likely to begin a soup kitchen or develop a shelter for the homeless than congregations that choose other heroes or no heroes at all.

Memory is not completely conscious and cannot be easily articulated. Some of the most compelling memories are carried in the rituals of worship, fellowship, and organizational activities. Every congregation tends to repeat and find strength in the rituals that reflect its unspoken commitment to its most comfortable style of doing such typical activities as praying, serving food, and raising money.

Memory is often the most dominant feature of a small congregation and is frequently the glue that holds the church together.[6] Such memories may make the congregation difficult for the newcomer to enter, especially if newcomers arrive with a "curate's complex," expecting to have something to offer even before they know the congregation. At the same time, congregational history can be mobilized for change when memories are chosen to fit the contemporary challenge and when the energizing spirit of adventure from the past is more important than merely repeating a particular pattern of behavior.

Thus, history is an ally toward change when congregational leaders select memories that help the congregation face the present. These memories frequently include invoking the names of "saints" and heroes in the congregation or the retelling of an event that is similar to the present challenge in its significant facts or in the spirit of the crisis that confronts the congregation.

### Vision as a Source for Change

Small congregations often see themselves so much on the margin of survival that they must struggle to find a vision for the future.[7] In reviewing different ways in which congregations

---

[6]For further discussion see Carl S. Dudley, *Making the Small Church Effective* (Nashville: Abingdon Press, 1978), especially chapters 5, 6, and 7.

[7]Robert D. Dale, *To Dream Again* (Nashville: Broadman Press, 1981).

experience a sense of time, Grierson concludes that churches generally live either in the past ("under time") or in the future ("beyond time"), but have difficulty living as if they could influence their own situation in the present time.[8]

Congregations that intentionally affect their times have a sense of purpose and a plan; they have a vision of what God is calling them to be and to do. Their vision is often grounded in the biblical promise and articulated only by a minority of members, but many more members feel the excitement and share the commitment. Thus the person who articulates the appropriate vision for the congregation becomes the leader and is both the cause and the result of a mobilized church; both the church and the leader are mutually empowered in the process. Pastors often report feeling a "second ordination" when the vision they have suggested is accepted and absorbed into the life of the congregation.

Congregational vision gains strength when it is consistent with congregational memory. It does not need to conform in all particulars (the times are always different), but it can carry on some basic congregational themes. This continuity of themes may be grounded in ethnic and cultural heritage. The pastor of a socially aggressive black church reports, "It should not be surprising that Melrose Temple's vision is so socially oriented. After all, its heritage as a black church in general and as an A.M.E. Zion church predisposes it to honor its role as a service agency for its people." Or the continuity of themes may be theological, as illustrated by the small, urban immigrant church that reported: "As the community began to change economically and ethnically, the church struggled with its mission. . . . A few voices cried, 'This is a Swedish church,' while other voices countered with, 'Our mission is to serve God in the midst of changes.' Both voices can be heard today, but the louder voice of change provided the congregation with a social justice ministry."

[8]Grierson, *Transforming a People of God,* especially chapter 4.

## Organizational Structure as a Source for Change

Imagination has power.[9] Churches are unlikely to accomplish what they cannot imagine themselves doing. Many possible changes in congregational life are frustrated by the absence of a common faith, a "con-fidence," among members to believe that they could accomplish something different. In order for the congregation to take on a new style or different responsibilities, the leadership or organizational support must be in place, or at least available. Memory may set the stage and vision may provide the direction and purpose, but a congregation can only respond when it believes that it has access to the decision-making structure and resources to follow through on its commitment.

Most small churches do less than they are capable of because they do not imagine that they have any "power." Edward Hassinger's classic studies[10] of small churches suggest that they use their smallness with great effectiveness—to reduce the expectations of denominational leaders and others who would make demands upon them. They can remember accomplishments of heroic proportions from the past when they were faced with impossible odds. But generally they avoid such an effort, lest it become habitual, forcing them to keep up the pace.

Organizational structure is the slowest of the three elements to develop. Leadership must be selected with care to reflect networks of trust within the congregation and nourished over time to develop the skills and inclination to lead in congregational decisions and actions. In comparison with organizational development, history is fun, and vision is dramatic. If new pastors needed to build a new congregational leadership team in each parish, it would probably take more time than most pastors are willing to spend. Fortunately, in most congregations

[9]A simple introduction can be found in Lewis S. Mudge, "Searching for Faith's Social Reality," *The Christian Century,* vol. 93 (September 1976), pp. 784–787.
[10]Edward Hassinger et al., *A Comparison of Rural Churches, The Church in Rural Missouri,* Research Bulletins 984, 999, and following (Columbia, Mo.: University of Missouri, College of Agriculture).

leadership is available to match the challenge, or they would not have survived until now. Most pastors need to learn the existing roles and relationships that hold together the leadership team of the church and then nourish both the confidence and the skills for stretching imaginations to meet new opportunities.

At the same time, many small churches are blessed with the negative impact of a "doubting Thomas," frequently the church treasurer. He (she) performs an essential function in challenging the congregation to produce the necessary resources to back up the decisions that they make. For some congregations, such doubters inhibit action. For other churches with more adventuresome imagination, the doubters (which are found in many roles) only spur the church to action—a result that may be consistent with the "best" in their congregational history. The leaders of many churches have given thanks for doubters, since, if their timing is right, they can energize the whole congregation to commitment simply by challenging the congregation's willingness to act.

Memory, vision, and organization—these three together form the elements of change within the life of the congregation.[11]

## Different Roles for Community Change

Congregations participate in change based upon their perception of their role in the community and their understanding of the issues to be addressed. Using the concepts of chapter 2, a Dominant church will approach community change through its congregational leadership drawn from the movers and shakers of the immediate community, while a Denominational congregation will seek to influence the community through the perspective of its denominational training, literature, and other resources.

[11]Note the similarities between these three elements and leadership definitions of Max Weber, for example, in *Max Weber on Charisma and Institution Building,* ed. S.N. Eisenstadt (Chicago:University of Chicago Press, 1968).

Distinctive congregations will be decisive either one way or the other: either they will withdraw from encounter with social and political issues, or they will actively be engaged in dealing with these issues as part of their sense of divine mission in the world. The focus of each response will be different. Those who withdraw will emphasize issues of private morality, such as the abuse of drugs, alcohol, and sexuality, and those who become involved in the world will place a greater emphasis on broad social issues such as racial discrimination, free speech, and world peace.

Typically, congregations will play different roles as they understand themselves, the issues, and the location of community resources and authority. Generally, the impact of small churches on community change can be clustered into three broad approaches.

## *Partner and Participant*

When Old First Church responded to a need among the elderly in the congregation for a hot meals program, it never occurred to them to limit the program to their members. Rather they collected all the available names of senior citizens living throughout their community. Each person was contacted and invited to participate, either in the church social hall or through a delivery service at home. The program took a year to launch because the old church building, although adequate for congregational purposes, did not meet state health and safety regulations for its new ministry. But the time was well spent mobilizing volunteers, many among the elderly, for the preparation, delivery, and maintenance of the hot meal program and upkeep of the building in which it was housed. From the beginning it was a success, which was no surprise since the "advisory board" for the program was peopled with the names of well-known and outstanding citizens. They considered it an honor to be asked.

Soon the program exceeded the facilities of the church, and it was moved into a public building in the community. There was no issue of church and state because the service program "belonged to the community," as one of its founders proudly announced. The cost was subsidized by this community's version of the United Fund when it outgrew the resources of the congregation, and a full-time cook was employed to coordinate the program. The cook prepared the basic meals, but the responsibility for garnishments and volunteers was rotated among several congregations of the community. The name was changed to reflect ecumenical participation, and an executive committee was made up of hard-working volunteers from each of the participating churches. But the advisory board remained as it had been from the beginning, dominated by the well-known names of Old First Church families.

Old First Church models a particular style of social ministry in which the church sees itself and its members as "at home" in the community. In this setting, the church itself may be the locale for a new ministry and the initiator of the change process. Members who have community leadership roles may carry the vision into the community, along with supporting memories and the confidence to act.

Many small churches have been vehicles for communities to expand their educational resources for children and adults, day-care for children, and hot meals for shut-ins and senior citizens. Acting in partnership with other churches, schools, and social agencies, small churches have often had the best location and strongest reputation to house ministries that materially change the life of the community. These may be limited by the available resources, but they do make a difference.

Old First Church was able to move the hot meals program to other space when they reached their own limits. By the nature of the service they were providing and the status of Old First Church in that community, they were able to broaden their base to include other congregations and expand the resources to attract financial support from the larger community. In many ways, as a Dominant church they assumed that they represented the community as seen in the way they went about developing the project from its inception.

## Service Broker and Resource

Zion Lutheran Church had a history of developing social ministries that stretched back almost one hundred years to its founding as a congregation serving a German immigrant community in a midwestern city. Throughout the years it had generated a school and provided a center of community life, and within its walls three generations of young Christians had entered the mainstream of American life. The community had changed in the last decade or so, and the condition of the building was not quite what it had been. However, pride in themselves remained in the strong cadre of members who still resided within the sound of its lovely carillon.

Zion church leaders began to feel that they had an obligation to their elderly members that they were unable to fulfill. They could not adequately help with the safety and the home maintenance of people who had been members all their lives. With denominational help, Zion Church developed a plan to convert an old school building a block away from the church into 205 units of housing for elderly citizens. Since the project was much too large for the congregation alone, Zion sparked the development of a Citizens Housing Committee and used its own property as collateral to launch the project. With help from federal agencies and national Lutheran Church resources, the community board has completed the project.

Zion Community Housing stands as a separate corporation, solvent but struggling, and remains a symbol of the commitment of one small church to use its resources and energy to strengthen the community in which it has served for nearly a century. For these kinds of issues, far too large for local churches to assume sole responsibility, a small church will sometimes serve as a broker or essential link in a network of resources, a center to help provide information and tangible aid to the local community in order to effect social change. In this process the church may be a catalyst in the chemistry of change, but it usually is not the primary institution in the change event.

Zion was more active than most, and the community honored that role in the project's name.

Sometimes small Denominational congregations have used church ties to find expertise for planning or to find financial resources through contacts with the private sector or government agencies. Some small churches have established local community boards to receive and administer these resources. Throughout the process, they lend the force of their reputation to build community confidence that change is possible.

## Protest and Prophetic Vision

Bethany is a small United Church of Christ congregation that has seen a parade of changing populations and retains a remnant of each. It is an activist church by any standard, taking on each new cause with all the relish of an old warrior who loves the battle but fears too many fights at any one time. The church is a dynamic paradox: prayerful but not liturgical; prophetic but unimpressed by preaching; service oriented but more interested in changing systems (such as education, housing, health care, and so forth); uninterested in recruiting members but attracting new people all the time; energized by issues but exhausted by programs.

Bethany United Church of Christ is a cross-cultural mix of every age, marital status, sexual orientation, race, class, and national background—but not every creed. In faith they are united to "love God and serve humanity," although they enjoy disagreeing over what that means at any given moment. They advocate for rights of gays, women, and minorities, and recently have taken stands on a nuclear weapons freeze and sanctuary protection for refugees. The press is familiar with their social concerns and often asks the pastor or leading members to provide a voice of Christian conscience in the midst of civic concerns. Last week, for example, they were in the news with a protest about the absence of housing for homeless people in the city. This week two of their members were arrested in a demonstration at the federal building to call attention to abuse of American power overseas. Both issues were included in the people's prayers in Sunday worship.

Because of their locations and the populations they serve, many small churches are uniquely situated to share the experience of alienation and to become the voice of those who are oppressed or victimized by our society. Although it is an uncomfortable role, many small churches have provided the prophetic voice that stands outside the power structure and affirms their identity in solidarity with those who are dispossessed, marginalized, and dehumanized by their social, economic, and spiritual conditions.

Representatives of such churches often gain a hearing far beyond their numbers, making significant contributions through the mass media, community studies, and ultimately legislative changes. In dealing with social needs, the leaders of small churches are often the central source of information and concern that can result in the development of such programs as housing loans, economic programs, and more sensitive care for the families of migrant workers.

In all three change processes, the leadership of the church must acclimate itself to different roles and recognize different pressures from the community. In the development of an educational program like Old First Church's, the congregation may see itself as a citizen and participant, even providing space for that program to be housed in the church. In the development of neighborhood housing ministries like Zion's, the church may be the quiet broker to link neighborhood leaders with the appropriate agencies that have the essential resources. In protesting the shape of society, as Bethany does, the church may see itself identified with the marginalized and oppressed people to become their advocate in their fight for physical resources and legislative change. Each is a different kind of social process and personal experience, but all precipitate community change.

We began in chapter 1 in the seminary classroom with a pastor telling of the three small churches that he serves— churches which in turn serve the needs of people who are in their communities. For us the phrase "who's there" is symbolic of the best in small churches—faithfully carrying out their vocation to serve "who's there" wherever they are.

## Questions for Discussion and Reflection

1. In the history of your church, what are the memories of community crises that needed congregational help? What caring did the church provide?

2. As you imagine the future of your area, what particular changes could strengthen the community quality of life? How could members of the church make a difference?

3. Does your church have the leadership, organization, and resources to make decisions that affect the area? Where might you begin?

4. What is your congregational sense of history—that the best is in the past, in the present, or yet to come? How can you mobilize your sense of history to strengthen your present ministry?

5. Can you name events in your congregational history in which your church has participated in social ministries as (a) partner and participant? (b) service broker and resource? (c) protester and prophetic voice? Are there people in the community who need you to serve in these ways now?